LIVING IN THE
ARTS AND CRAFTS STYLE

LIVING IN THE
ARTS AND CRAFTS STYLE

Your Complete Home Decorating Guide

BY

CHARLOTTE
KELLEY

CHRONICLE BOOKS

SAN FRANCISCO

First Chronicle Books LLC paperback edition,
published in 2006.
First published in a workbook edition in 2001
by Quarto Publishing plc.

Library of Congress Cataloging-in-Publication
Data available.

ISBN-10 0-8118-5363-2
ISBN-13 978-0-8118-5363-7

Manufactured in China.

This book was designed and produced by
Quarto Publishing plc
6 Blundell Street
London N7 9BH

Senior project editor   Nicolette Linton
Senior art editor   Penny Cobb
Designer   Tanya Devonshire-Jones
Text editors   Morag Lyall, Pat Farrington
Picture Research   Laurent Boubounelle
Photography Paul Forrester
Illustrator   Coral Mula
Indexer   Pamela Ellis

Art director   Moira Clinch
Publisher   Piers Spence

Distributed in Canada by Raincoast Books
9050 Shaughnessy Street
Vancouver, British Columbia
V6P 6E5

10 9 8 7 6 5 4 3 2 1

Chronicle Books LLC
85 Second Street
San Francisco, California
94105

www.chroniclebooks.com

A QUARTO BOOK

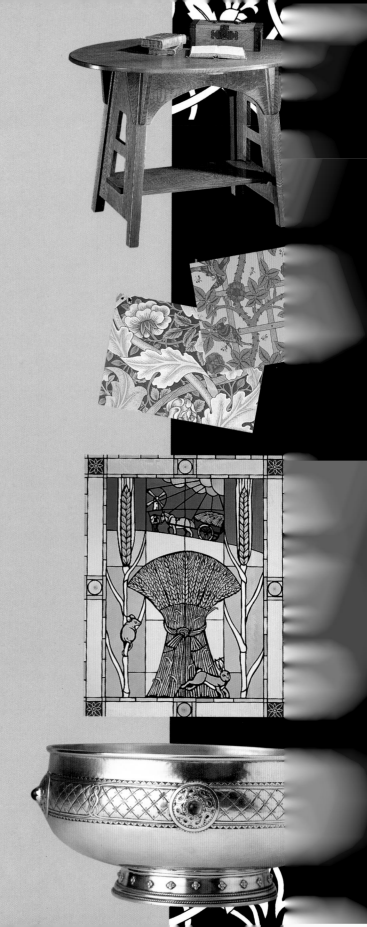

CONTENTS

INTRODUCTION

Arts and Crafts style is as compelling and relevant today as it was in its heyday in the mid-nineteenth and early twentieth centuries. Much more than just a style of decoration, the Arts and Crafts Movement began as one of social reform, and the Arts and Crafts style echoes the Movement's founding principles of integrity and social responsibility. With its hallmark simple designs, beautiful materials, and honest craftsmanship, it is no wonder that the look remains an enduring cornerstone of modern interior design to this day.

No single style is entirely representative of the Movement, which may be one reason for its enduring popularity. The Arts and Crafts look suits a broad range of tastes and homes, while the styles mingle well with more modern design elements. The Japanese lines of Frank Lloyd Wright or Charles Rennie Mackintosh sit perfectly with a minimalist urban decor, while William Morris's floral textiles and cottage furniture bring softness and warmth to a family home. Similarly, the Mission and Prairie styles associated with Gustav Stickley and Greene & Greene are as at home in a country ranch as they are in a city loft.

The roots of the Arts and Crafts Movement lie in the aesthetic approach to interior design and interest in social reform that originated with the reformers and writers August Pugin and John Ruskin. Changes brought about by the Industrial Revolution in mid-Victorian England inspired a quest for a return to simplicity, honesty, and beauty. As people flooded from the countryside into cities to work in newly built factories, they left behind traditions of home and family life. Followers of the Movement believed that the factory system stripped workers of their dignity, and that a return to true craftsmanship and its artisan way of life was paramount to a healthy society. Designers like William Morris, C.F.A. Voysey, and Charles Rennie Mackintosh founded a whole new

"The great advantage and charm of the Morrisian method is that it lends itself to either simplicity or splendour. You might be almost as plain as Thoreau, with a rush-bottomed chair, piece of matting, and oaken trestle table; or you might have gold and lustre (the choice ware of William de Morgan) gleaming from the sideboard, and jewelled light in the windows, and walls hung with arras tapestry."
Walter Crane

Gustav Stickley's Craftsman style of furniture and lighting is beautifully complemented by the neutral walls, wooden flooring, and Indian drugget rug.

design ethos that rejected the overly ornate decorations and machine-made furniture, textiles, and ornaments of the Victorian era. Morris revived traditional weaving, dyeing, and textile printing – crafts that had already succumbed to the lure of industrialization – and William de Morgan's handmade luster-glazed ceramics with Persian, medieval, and floral motifs were works of art in themselves.

Once these designs were brought to the United States by style ambassadors such as playwright Oscar Wilde and retail giant Arthur Lasenby Liberty, American designers and craftsmen took the ideas to a new level. In the second half of the nineteenth century, America was experiencing its own industrial boom, giving rise to a new moneyed middle class. Designers like Gustav Stickley, Greene & Greene, and Frank Lloyd Wright developed the Arts and Crafts style, drawing inspiration from the Shaker Movement and the crafts of the indigenous American people. And unlike the British Movement, American designers embraced the machine, which enabled more people to buy Arts and Crafts pieces – real design and quality for the masses.

> "Have nothing in your houses that you do not know to be useful or believe to be beautiful."
> **William Morris**

Affluent families commissioned architects to build the most impressive houses affordable, and these were built with local wood and stone to blend into the surrounding landscape. Rooms were open and spacious, enabling family and friends to gather together in comfort. Dust-gatherers such as knick-knacks and heavy curtains were discouraged, and fresh air was recommended for good health. Sleeping porches and cushioned window seats were built to allow access to light and scenery. The natural theme spread to walls and floors: polished wood paneling and flooring

William Morris's original design for Avon chintz, c.1886.

Frank Lloyd Wright's geometric style of furniture, lighting, and stained glass dominates the interior of the Meyer May house in Michigan (U.S.A.), which he completed in 1909.

teamed with wallpaper featuring floral motifs. Light muslin, linen, and cotton drapes with stylized repeats brought a touch of nature into the home, and beautifully crafted furniture revealed the grain of the local wood, such as American oak.

Although the Arts and Crafts Movement waned in popularity after the First World War, the 1980s saw a revival in the Movement's craftsmanship and materials. Collectors began to snap up originals such as Stickley armchairs and Craftsman or Tiffany lamps, and these days original pieces are rare and expensive. However, the Arts and Craft look is still widely available to those outside of the collectors' market. There are many designers today who have taken the Arts and Crafts style as an inspiration or starting point, and these pieces of furniture, fabrics, rugs, and ornaments are much easier to find. Reproduction furniture is available from suppliers, and original designs of wallpaper and carpets are still in production today.

Tiffany style standard lamp with popular bamboo stained glass motif and brass base.

Today's Arts and Crafts interior begins with simple wooden flooring softened with sisal, jute, rush, or coir matting for hard-wearing areas, and oriental, persian or native American rugs for more colorful accents. Walls paneled up to the dado rail or shoulder height warm up or lighten the room, depending on whether the wood is left natural and polished, or painted white. Above the paneling, walls may be painted white or a natural shade, or covered in

Oak Arts and Crafts dining table and chairs suit this airy octagonal room in an English house designed by C.F.A. Voysey.

wallpaper with repeating floral motifs. Windows simply decorated with lightweight drapes – muslin, cotton, or linen panels hung from wooden poles – add another layer of texture to the primarily neutral walls.

This simple canvas allows furniture to stand out as a feature in its own right. The beauty of the wood grain and the excellent craftsmanship make Arts and Crafts furniture truly wonderful to behold – if not entirely comfortable to sit on. Fabric-covered or leather-upholstered cushions soften hard wooden seats. Authentic Arts and Crafts upholstery fabrics are widely available today through suppliers such as Sanderson's or Burrows, and cushions fashioned from these classic patterns add authenticity to a room.

Lamps have always been a hallmark of Arts and Crafts decoration and numerous modern designers have adapted or reproduced the Craftsman, Mackintosh, and Tiffany styles. A standard lamp in a corner and a strategically placed table lamp add pools of light to a room and can highlight favorite ornaments. Paintings or photographs hung in clusters near a lamp can make an interesting focal point, as can collections of Arts and Crafts metalware picture frames, jugs, or vases. Unlike Victorian rooms, which were awash with knick-knacks, the Arts and Crafts ideal was to use only objects that were deemed to be both beautiful and necessary.

The Movement borrowed extensively from other cultures

"The root of all reform lies in the individual and (that) the life of the individual is shaped mainly by home surroundings."
Gustav Stickley

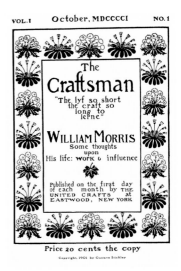

First issue of *The Craftsman* published by Gustav Stickley in October 1901.

Stickley settle upholstered in burgundy leather, still available today from the Stickley workshop in New York State (U.S.A.).

and periods, owing debts to India, Japan, the Middle East, Scandinavia, Celtic Ireland, Byzantium, as well as medieval Europe and Renaissance Italy (for example, Indian carpets, Japanese design, Scandinavian colors, Celtic and medieval motifs). Today, the ease of international travel makes it ever more possible to bring home ornaments, rugs, and cushions that resonate with the Arts and Crafts aesthetic.

"New artisans continue to build on the ideals and designs of the original Movement to create beautiful and affordable pieces."

For those unable to buy original pieces, many designers and suppliers in the United States produce Arts and Crafts-inspired pieces or reproductions. In fact, there are those who see the current revival more as an evolution of the Arts and Crafts style. New artisans continue to build on the ideals and designs of the original Movement to create beautiful and affordable pieces.

There is no doubt that the Arts and Crafts Movement succeeded on a design level, although given that its products remained largely the province of the middle-class home, the Movement's socialist ethic was not entirely fulfilled. Thanks to the availability of quality goods and higher standards of living today, we now have the opportunity to redress this balance.

Reproduction William de Morgan tile designs are available from specialist suppliers.

William Morris's wallpaper designs are still in production by companies such as Sanderson's.

William Morris's Tulip and Rose pattern is now available as a tapestry cushion.

HOW TO USE THIS BOOK

Before you plan your scheme, be inspired by the original and modern Arts and Crafts-style rooms on the feature spreads in this book. Then pinpoint the different colors, patterns, ornaments, and styles of furniture available to create your chosen look.

Feature spread A full-color, inspirational photograph of an Arts and Crafts-style room, with captions explaining the different elements in the picture.

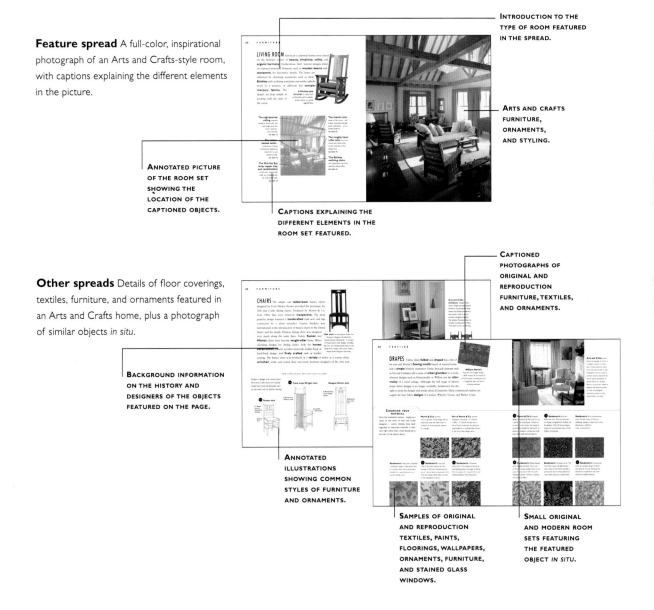

INTRODUCTION TO THE TYPE OF ROOM FEATURED IN THE SPREAD.

ARTS AND CRAFTS FURNITURE, ORNAMENTS, AND STYLING.

ANNOTATED PICTURE OF THE ROOM SET SHOWING THE LOCATION OF THE CAPTIONED OBJECTS.

CAPTIONS EXPLAINING THE DIFFERENT ELEMENTS IN THE ROOM SET FEATURED.

CAPTIONED PHOTOGRAPHS OF ORIGINAL AND REPRODUCTION FURNITURE, TEXTILES, AND ORNAMENTS.

Other spreads Details of floor coverings, textiles, furniture, and ornaments featured in an Arts and Crafts home, plus a photograph of similar objects *in situ*.

BACKGROUND INFORMATION ON THE HISTORY AND DESIGNERS OF THE OBJECTS FEATURED ON THE PAGE.

ANNOTATED ILLUSTRATIONS SHOWING COMMON STYLES OF FURNITURE AND ORNAMENTS.

SAMPLES OF ORIGINAL AND REPRODUCTION TEXTILES, PAINTS, FLOORINGS, WALLPAPERS, ORNAMENTS, FURNITURE, AND STAINED GLASS WINDOWS.

SMALL ORIGINAL AND MODERN ROOM SETS FEATURING THE FEATURED OBJECT *IN SITU*.

Chapter **1**

WALLS AND FLOORS

**Walls and floors are a backdrop for the furniture,
textiles, and ornaments displayed in the home.
The basic components of Arts and Crafts style
include wooden floors, rugs, tiles, paneling
and wallpaper.**

BEDROOM

Arts and Crafts bedrooms, unlike Victorian bedchambers, were decorated in a **simple** and **light** style to provide a **peaceful haven** for sleep and, if necessary, convalescence or periods of **rest**. Free-standing furniture was encouraged, so that rooms were easier to keep clean and dust-free. Heavy velvet drapes and bedlinens were replaced with **muslins** and light chintzes, and dark decorations gave way to **plain walls** and light wallpapers. Bedcovers were often plain, **embroidered**, or were pretty, hand-made **patchwork quilts**.

The color green was popular, as it complemented white walls and textiles with floral designs.

Oak wardrobe with heart-shaped Ruskin enamels, stylized lily fruitwood panels, and cruciform ring handles. Although Arts and Crafts designers invented built-in wardrobes, free-standing furniture was encouraged to make thorough cleaning and dusting possible.
SEE PAGE 94

A Liberty's rush-seated beech side chair fits neatly in the corner of the room.
SEE PAGE 64

An oak bedside cabinet is the perfect place to put a table lamp and flowers or books.
SEE PAGE 94

Pine chests are useful for storing bedlinens, quilts, and blankets – especially in summer. They also provide an extra surface for books and accessories.
SEE PAGE 98

Brass beds can be bought from furniture suppliers, or you can even scour antique markets for originals. Painted or wooden beds are also an option.
SEE PAGE 94

Plain, white walls and ceiling are the perfect backdrop to an Arts and Crafts bedroom. The green-painted beams add a colorful accent.
SEE PAGE 18

Mackintosh-style cushions are still available from specialist suppliers and the Glasgow School of Art in Scotland.
SEE PAGE 52

A patchwork quilt adds a cozy feel to a bedroom, and the fact that it is hand-crafted fits in well with the Arts and Crafts ideal.
SEE PAGE 52

PAINT

White distempered **walls** were a feature of William Morris's rural retreats and were also popular with American Arts and Crafts designers. Should you opt for plain **white** walls you will need to find a pure shade. **Distemper** has a unique formula which can offer a very appealing chalky finish. Color paints are a means of generating a particular atmosphere in a room. Ideally, **color** tones should be based on **natural** hues such as fresh green, serene blue, warm russet, or classic cream.

A fresh lick of paint can make all the difference to a room. Choose one of the colors shown below for the perfect Arts and Crafts canvas.

CHOOSING PAINTS

White painted walls provide a neutral backdrop to an Arts and Crafts interior, but color in a room can add warmth or atmosphere. Keep to natural tones and you can't go far wrong.

White

Chalk white

Yellow

Ochre

Pink

Red ochre

Red

Purple

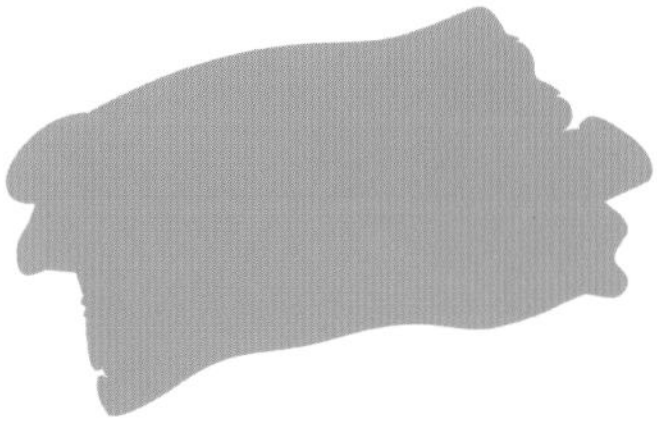

A fine example of a carefully chosen wall finish, which is in complete harmony with the upholstery, the simple wooden floorboards, and the Sussex bench. Morris advised painting wood-work white which, as you can see here, adds an additional element of freshness and light to the scheme.

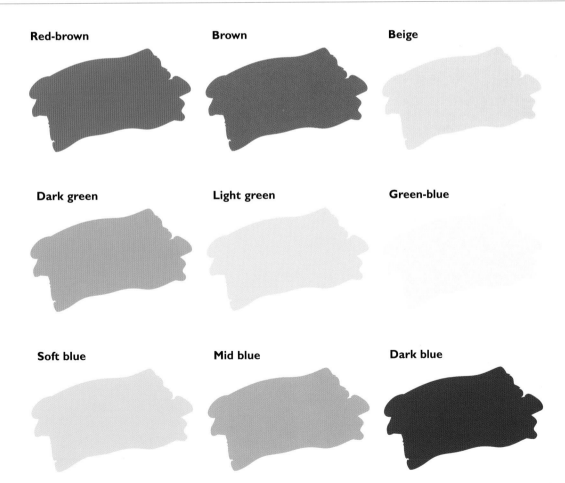

Red-brown

Brown

Beige

Dark green

Light green

Green-blue

Soft blue

Mid blue

Dark blue

LIVING ROOM

Arts and Crafts designers would have hated the modern practice of matching every item of fabric and wallpaper in an interior. They thought nothing of **mixing** different **patterns** in a living room, as long as these were **selected** and **balanced** carefully to avoid visual confusion. This approach is evident in Morris's London home where a number of **different patterns** are juxtaposed in a **harmonious** manner. Morris's Willow wallpaper design and Chrysanthemum fabric for the drapes are **complemented** by Delft tiles, oriental rugs, and decorative furniture covers.

Floral patterned wallpaper – such as Willow Bough and Morris's small-flower creations – were a popular choice for living rooms and bedrooms.

Evenlode fabric, 1883. This was one of the first fabrics to be printed at Merton Abbey using the indigo discharge method.
SEE PAGE 46

Decorative tiles designed by Arts and Crafts ceramicist, William de Morgan.
SEE PAGE 38

Sussex arm-chair. One of the most popular furniture designs produced by Morris & Co., it works well in an informal and formal interior.
SEE PAGE 64

Willow wall-paper, perhaps the most popular of Morris's designs, inspired by a walk by his stream with his daughter.
SEE PAGE 22

William Morris and Jane Burden portraits As this was Morris's London living room, there are a number of portraits of Morris and his wife, Jane.

Dutch Delft tiles. Morris had a deep affection for these folk designs in distinctive blue on a white tin-glazed background.
SEE PAGE 38

Brer Rabbit fabric design. Philip Webb contributed the bird motifs in this design.
SEE PAGE 46

WALLPAPERS

Arts and Crafts wallpapers are characterized by **stylized** decorative forms inspired by **nature**. Through the use of continuous flowing lines and carefully organized **repeats**, William **Morris** was able to convey the spontaneous growth of nature in his wallpaper designs, producing over 41 of them during his illustrious career. This success had a notable influence on other **followers** of the Arts and Crafts Movement: C.F.A. **Voysey** and Walter Crane in England, the Wiener Werkstätte in Austria, and

Wallpaper design by the Silver Studio, c.1890. The Silver Studio, founded by Arthur Silver, was responsible for some of Liberty's most popular and characteristic wallpaper designs, especially the famous Peacock Feather.

CHOOSING WALLPAPER

Wallpaper is only part of the decorative scheme and must be chosen in the context of the decor and proportions of the room in question. A horizontal pattern adds a touch of stability to large walls whereas a vertical pattern adds a sense of gravitas and formality to low walls.

William Morris's Willow wallpaper, 1874. Willow still remains one of the most popular of Morris's wallpaper designs. It can be particularly effective in a bedroom or a bathroom thanks to its tranquil and fresh nature.

William Morris's Pomegranate or Fruit print is the most sophisticated of Morris's early wallpaper designs. He employed the branches of a fruit tree to articulate the repeat patterns of the design.

William Morris's Daisy. The first wallpaper design to be issued by Morris & Co. in 1862. The pattern is composed of alternate repeating plant motifs.

William Morris's small white and pink floral design. Morris's love of gardening and careful observation of British hedgerows is particularly evident in this modest yet beautifully constructed design.

William Morris's Trellis design, 1864. Although this was Morris's first wallpaper pattern, it was the third design issued. It is said to have been inspired by the rose trellis that ran along the garden at the Red House.

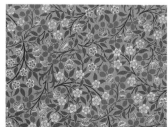

Fruit wallpaper designed by Morris and now supplied by Sanderson's. An early customer of Morris & Co., who decorated his living room with this design, observed proudly to a visitor that the flora on the walls of the room in which they sat seemed "as if it was all a-growing."

William Morris's Acanthus Leaves, wild rose on crimson background. Morris was particularly fond of the curving leaves of the acanthus, which he used over and over again, both as a main and subsidiary motif.

William Morris's powdered wallpaper, 1874. An uncharacteristically naive design. Morris later abstracted the background pattern for his famous Willow designs.

York wallpaper, 1885. A fresh, tranquil pattern that reveals a fusion of the style of Morris's and Voysey's wallpaper designs.

William Morris's Trellis design, 1864. The structure of this design around the wooden trellis is very effective. It is thought that the birds were the work of Morris's colleague, Philip Webb.

William Morris's Tulip design, 1875. Although this seems to be a simple design, it uses many different colors, and 18 wooden blocks were required to complete the pattern.

C.F.A. Voysey's "Let Us Prey" design shows his characteristic simplicity of line. He often features a bird motif, as in this print featuring a cat and bird repeat.

American designers such as Candace Wheeler. **Wallpapers** from the great Arts and Crafts designers are still **available** as machine or hand-prints (the more expensive option). They can be used as a **continuous wall covering**, or above a dado rail, or even on a single wall. When choosing a wallpaper design, it's important to ensure that the overall effect is in **harmony** with your furniture and other decorations. Try to envisage the design in accordance with the room's **proportions;** the larger the room the greater the size of repeats and the bolder the patterns you can get away with. Don't overwhelm a smaller room

Silver Studio's Tulips print attributed to J.I. Kay, c.1898. Designs such as this one were sold by Silver Studio to leading manufacturers and stores in the U.K., the U.S.A., and Continental Europe.

Burrows & Co.'s Chrysanthemum print. A simple and more tranquil interpretation of Morris's original design. The lacy leaves and flowing flowers reveal a Japanese influence.

Burrows & Co.'s Persis wall print in pale gold – a companion design to Persis Frieze. The main eucalyptus motif is a particularly good background against which to hang artwork.

Walter Crane's Francesca design. British-born designer Crane was one of the most effective promoters of the Arts and Crafts style in America, as well as a highly successful illustrator of children's books.

Burrows & Co.'s Lily and Rose. A fluid Scottish design with tendrils of lilies climbing in a diagonal line through conventionalized rose blossoms.

Burrows & Co.'s Gingko Leaf. A Japanese wallpaper design first published in New York in 1895. Japanese designs and motifs were popular with Arts and Crafts designers because of their linear simplicity and color tones.

Morris's Honeysuckle wallpaper design provides a fitting backdrop to a tiled fireplace featuring an oak mantel clock, c.1900, and a collection of metalware jugs and candlesticks.

H. & H. Birge & Sons' highly textured wallpaper with embossed silver is designed along the lines of the Art Nouveau style of Continental Europe. Although the nature of this design would perhaps prove too elaborate for an entire wall area, it could be integrated with paler walls to provide a strong decorative focus.

Burrows & Co.'s Summer Street Damask print, attributed to John Dando Sedding. This subtle design of figs and fig leaves reveals a stylistic integration of the Arts and Crafts and Art Nouveau styles.

Sanderson's Jasmine print. The loose and meandering structure of this design provides a naturalistic effect, in that there is a distinct impression of organic and spontaneous growth.

Sanderson's Jasmine print. Many of Morris's wallpaper designs work well in a number of different color combinations. The crossing of darker pink tones with lighter ones from behind creates a sense of depth.

Burrows & Co.'s Depden design. This design would be partic-ularly effective as a dado, or as a band or ornament – wherever a simple repeating design is required.

Sanderson's Compton print is available in different colors. The strong pattern would suit a tall hallway or staircase where the eye naturally looks upward.

Sanderson's Compton print. Although this pattern was originally designed by Morris for use as a fabric, it works equally well as wallpaper.

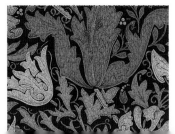

with your **choice** of wallpaper. To gain some idea how different patterns will work together, it is often useful to assemble **samples** of wallpaper before committing yourself on a larger scale. **Explore** a number of different **patterns** and make sure that you view the samples by both natural and artificial **light**. Designers sometimes used a **frieze** above the paneling and below the ceiling line. The inspiration for the use of the **decorative** friezes came from the painted or stenciled borders that were favored in medieval and Renaissance houses.

Swan Frieze by Voysey, the bird and animal designer par excellence of the nineteenth century. These swans, although highly naturalistic, are depicted in a simple, flat, stylized form, which is not too "dishonestly" three-dimensional as was the case with many earlier Victorian frieze designs.

Sanderson's Fruit print is built up from the repetition of four rectangular elements. For such an early design, it appears relatively complex thanks to the strong diagonal element of the branches and leaves.

Sanderson's Willow Bough print. Morris's daughter May recorded that this popular design was inspired by a walk by their stream, when Morris pointed out to her the detail and variety in the leaf forms.

Sanderson's Honeysuckle print. May, a talented designer in her own right, favored this design as it was the "most mysterious and poetic – the very symbol of a garden tangle."

Sanderson's Arbutus print. As its name implies, this is a highly verdant design and would help to achieve a formal, yet very fresh effect within a dining or sitting room.

Sanderson's Vine print. A bold design with soft, easy lines based on the naturally trailing branches of the vine plant. As there is plenty of movement in this pattern, it is equally suitable for a large or small wall.

Sanderson's Savernake print. A lighter and less elaborate interpretation of Morris's original, highly colored Snakeshead design.

Iris Frieze by Bradbury and Bradbury provides a perfect cut-off point between the lower oak paneling and the wooden beamed ceiling in this American dining room.

Burrows & Co.'s Persis Wall. An anonymous English design representative of the early Arts and Crafts movement. The dancing sprays of eucalyptus leaves would provide a decorative focus within a room or hallway broken up by many windows and doors.

Burrows & Co.'s Chauncy Frieze. A simple meandering design based on natural foliage motifs which works particularly well if applied in conjunction with plain whitewashed walls and in a room with exposed woodwork. Like the Persis Frieze, this design is available in a number of colors.

DINING ROOM

Morris and his associates were keen supporters of wooden paneling. They believed it to be a wall surface which formed "a **faultless background,** composed, **dignified**, and **reposeful** as the heart could wish," and although it does not have the suggestiveness and variety of color that tapestry possesses, it has "a **poetry** of its own, a grave and **quiet** charm which is the essence of decorative content." Wooden paneling worked well in dining rooms – an important room for the **family**, as this is where everyone gathered at least once a day.

If possible, choose wooden panels that are native to your area, such as oak or elm.

The white-beamed border adds a lighter touch to the heavily paneled oak walls.
SEE PAGE 18

These beautiful built-in display cabinets provide a decorative focus within the vast expanse of oak paneling.
SEE PAGE 86

Inlaid mother-of-pearl gives an Art Nouveau feel to the brick-colored hearth tiles.
SEE PAGE 38

Wooden lighting accessories were a development particular to the Arts and Crafts movement in America.
SEE PAGE 120

The wooden-paneled walls evoke a log cabin feel traditional to American Craftsman architecture and interior design.
SEE PAGE 30

Signs of craftsmanship, such as the metal bolts of the chair, were left exposed with pride by Arts and Crafts designers.
SEE PAGE 64

PANELING

Wooden paneling or **wainscoting** was a common feature of housing until the end of the eighteenth century and came into its own as a natural interior **feature** with the American Arts and Crafts Movement. Designers celebrated the **natural** and honest tones of wood or painted it **white** to add a touch of light to an interior. The type of **wood** varied according to the location of the house and the inclination of the architect or householder. **Oak** and native redwood were favored by Frank Lloyd Wright and the Greene brothers for interior **beams** and paneling.

Your local carpenter will be able to advise you which wood is best for your room. Or you could paint or stain your panels for a different look.

PANELS FOR YOUR ROOM

To create a wooden paneling scheme, choose a wood that is natural in tone and that suits the proportions of the room. Oak panels are expensive, but cheaper woods such as pine or deal could be stained green or painted white. You could even use a veneer instead.

English oak

Fumed oak

Southern yellow pine

American red oak

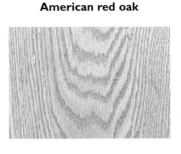

American white ash

Maple

Elm

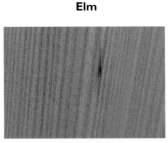

American walnut

Oak paneling creates a warm surround for the stunning tiled fireplace in Debenham House, London (England) designed by Halsey Ricardo.

The painted paneling acts as a perfect cut-off point between the ornate Honeysuckle wallpaper and the vivid, upholstered sofa.

STENCILS

Stenciling is a **print-making** technique that allows a design to be repeated on almost any surface. **Wall** and **furniture** stenciling was particularly popular in America and Europe during the nineteenth century before the mass production of wallpaper, especially as part of the overall decor of **bedrooms.** There is a wide range of pre-cut **stencils** on the market and the technique itself is relatively **quick and easy** to master.

Choose a color that will suit your scheme to create an individual look from a pre-cut stencil.

USING STENCILS

Stencil designs are an economic and versatile form of decoration. Carefully executed stenciling can offer an almost identical effect to more expensive runs of printed paper. Your local craft store will be able to advise you on the technique.

Ivy

Peacock

Leafy branch

Willow and flower

Roses

Heart and leaves

Tree

Flowers and leaves

Stag

Bamboo

Lettered stenciling adds a unique touch to the area between the decorative ceiling and the plain white walls of this bedroom in Holland House, London (England).

Leaves

Sun

Tulip group

Daisy girl

Flower

Rose

Pot and plant

Orchard

Trellis

HALLWAY

Gamble House in California (U.S.A.) – one of the finest examples of Prairie-style architecture, created by **Greene & Greene** – has impressed countless designers and architects since it was built in 1909. The **wood-lined walls** and **wooden flooring** give the hallway a feeling of airy space, and the large **oriental rugs** and **stained glass** front doors add color and **warmth**. The hall is the first room that most visitors see, and this is as **impressive** today as it must have been in its heyday.

Sisal matting is an attractive alternative to wooden floors, especially where you may prefer more warmth underfoot, like in the bedroom. Don't use sisal or rush in the bathroom or kitchen – they don't react well to water.

A Japanese influence figures heavily in Gamble House's architecture and interior decoration. The ceiling light in the hallway is similar to a Japanese lantern.
SEE PAGE 120

The art glass front door by Emil Lange features a jewel-like tree of life design inspired by Californian oak trees. The whole room glows when the sun shines through the glass in the mornings.
SEE PAGE 118

A Craftsman-style table lamp with stained glass pattern sheds a pool of light on the wooden paneling and hall table, where visitors would have left their calling cards.
SEE PAGE 120

Greene & Greene chairs, upholstered in leather, provide a welcome seating area for visitors.
SEE PAGE 64

Wooden floors – despite their innate beauty – are often softened by boldly designed and highly colored rugs. Make sure they are laid securely.
SEE PAGE 36

FLOORING

Plain polished **floorboards** complement an Arts and Crafts interior, and **woven** or **rush** rugs soften the look. Morris & Co.'s original woven rugs are now collectors' items, but modern versions of the designs are available. Gustav Stickley produced a range of **zigzag** rugs which proved hugely popular. When choosing a rug or carpet, keep to a **floral** or geometric design. Modern **alternatives** are kelims and dhurries from India and the Middle East, Native American Indian Navaho rugs, and knotted rugs.

Morris reproduction rug by Designer's Forum. Although Morris moved his loom from Hammersmith (England) to the Merton Abbey works in 1881, his hand-knotted rugs, made with naturally dyed wools, were always known as Hammersmith carpets.

CHOICES FOR FLOORING

Older floorboards are rare and highly sought after, but hardwood and softwood laminates provide an affordable alternative. Sisal and rush matting, and rugs work well to soften the boards.

Natural wooden floor

Whitewashed wooden floor

Sisal matting

Polished wooden floor

Stained wooden floor

Rush matting

The wooden floorboards shown here not only provide an appropriate rustic feel to the room, but also offset the dark olive-green walls, which would otherwise be rather oppressive. The stripped pine door and furniture also complement the natural atmosphere of the room.

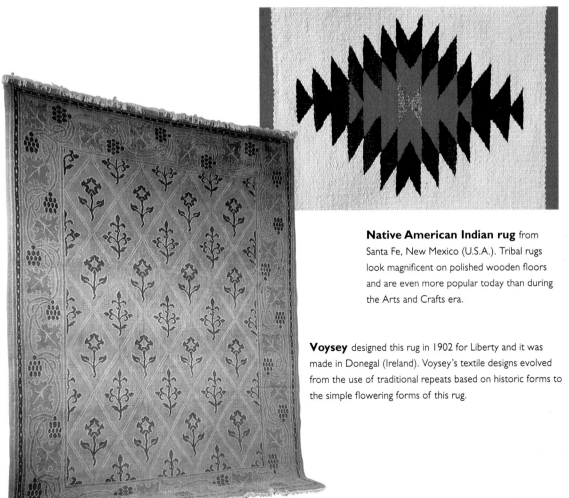

Native American Indian rug from Santa Fe, New Mexico (U.S.A.). Tribal rugs look magnificent on polished wooden floors and are even more popular today than during the Arts and Crafts era.

Voysey designed this rug in 1902 for Liberty and it was made in Donegal (Ireland). Voysey's textile designs evolved from the use of traditional repeats based on historic forms to the simple flowering forms of this rug.

TILES

Arts and Crafts designers made it acceptable to cover a large **wall** area with tiles as part of a **decorative** scheme. William de Morgan, an associate of Morris, produced **art tiles** that were available on both sides of the Atlantic and proved especially suitable for **fireplace** surrounds. Art tiles were highly **popular in America**, where at least 50 tile companies were founded between 1875 and 1920.

William de Morgan
Persian Moffat patterned tile produced at the ceramic works, Merton Abbey (England). Floral designs were rarely used on tiles until William de Morgan revived an interest in Islamic-inspired floral designs in the 1870s.

AUTHENTIC DESIGNS

Tiles by William de Morgan can be identified by a bold use of luster glaze — usually with a copper or silver film — and strong designs inspired by natural and decorative motifs.

William de Morgan Animals frequently appeared in de Morgan's tiles, like this porcupine in red luster on pottery.

William de Morgan This buff earthenware tile depicts a dragon, reflecting the interest in medieval fables at the time.

William de Morgan This earthenware tile with luster glaze was decorated with dark blue bird-like dragons.

William de Morgan A Persian-style flower adorns this tile most likely produced at his workshop in Chelsea (England).

William de Morgan An abstract floral pattern in blue and brown decorates this earthenware tile by de Morgan.

Halsey Ricardo worked closely with William de Morgan to produce the exotic color scheme of this tiled hallway. The marble skirtings and pillar, combined with the jewel-like quality of the indigo tiles, give this hallway an Islamic feel.

Artichoke design tiles adorn the base of the fireplace in the Green Room at Kelmscott Manor, Morris's rural retreat in Gloucestershire (England).

William de Morgan tiled frieze from Leighton House, London (England), which houses the famous Arab Hall. Oriental accents in decoration were common in the second half of the nineteenth century.

Today, **handpainted** tiles in the Arts and Crafts style can be purchased at a relatively reasonable cost. Tiled walls are a highly **practical choice** for kitchens and bathrooms, and the odd pictorial design can offset any of the blandness a plain run of tiles could offer. **Flora** and **fauna** motifs are still popular choices – and **blue** is the dominant color.

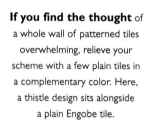

If you find the thought of a whole wall of patterned tiles overwhelming, relieve your scheme with a few plain tiles in a complementary color. Here, a thistle design sits alongside a plain Engobe tile.

MODERN TILES

The Arts and Crafts look is popular for tiles, and some suppliers are especially thorough in their research into the correct designs and glazes to use. Flora and fauna predominate, and the patterned tiles are attractive as a fireplace surround or a splash-back above a kitchen or bedroom sink.

Nine Square Bough William Morris was keen on blue on white for domestic interiors and glazed plain white tiles with enamel.

Fruit Tree Morris's wallpaper designs were often used for other purposes, such as on glazed tiles.

Fish William de Morgan's fish design can be used singly, with plain Engobe tiles, as above, or as a frieze.

Findon Daisy Designed by Morris, this tile looks especially good in a fireplace or above a sink in a bedroom.

Magpie Philip Webb originally designed this bird, which is now being reproduced by a modern supplier.

The Gothic revival assisted the rediscovery of geometric tile designs, which are still highly popular today. They are particularly practical for large tiled spaces such as floors and bathroom walls and can be beautifully complemented by pictorial tiles such as these Ironbridge tiles. The Encaustic Tile Company at Ironbridge (England) remains in production today.

A sympathetically designed reproduction fireplace with Morris-style tiles can be the focal point of your living room, dining room, or even your bedroom or bathroom. There are many styles of tile that would suit this type of fireplace.

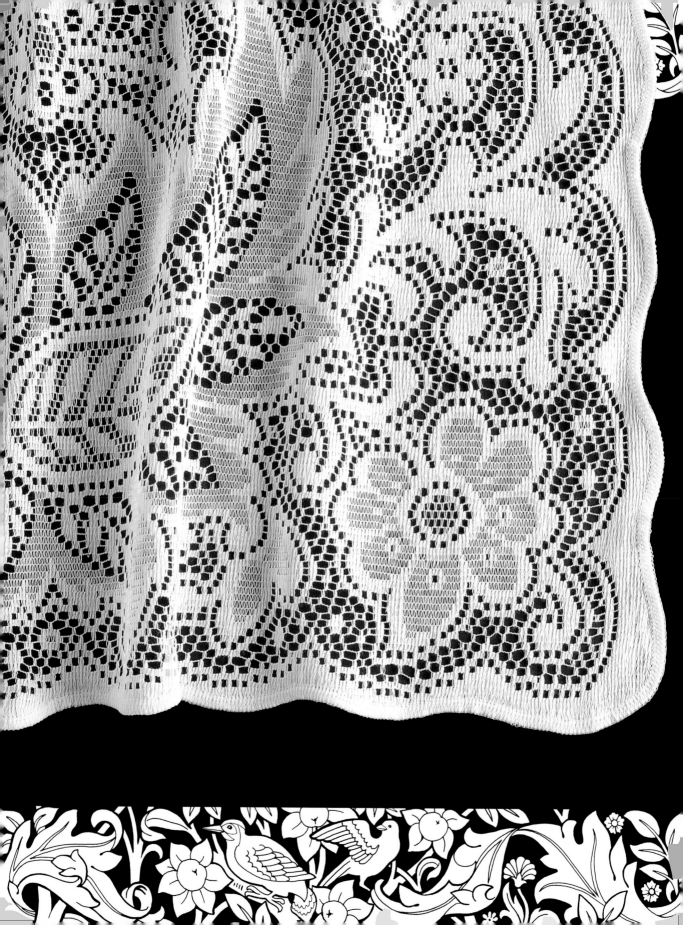

Chapter **2**

TEXTILES
Arts and Crafts textiles suit many interior schemes and are still extremely popular. The king of Arts and Crafts textile design, William Morris, combined natural fabrics, handcrafting techniques, and stylized designs to produce timeless patterns that had a huge impact on drapes, wall hangings, and upholstery of the day.

LIVING ROOM

Although William Morris never attempted to imitate nature, it was certainly one of his chief desires to **incorporate nature** into the domestic interior. In this living room, the **natural form** of his drape fabric – Bird and Anemone – is enhanced by the **pale green** wall paint, **white floorboards,** and the **simple** arrangement of **furniture**.

Overall, there is a verdant and organic quality which bridges the gap between the **interior** and **exterior world,** which would prove particularly **soothing** in an urban environment.

Textile designs like Bird and Anemone are available in different colors, such as red (above) and green (main picture).

Bird and Anemone drape fabric, a variation on Morris's original, famous Bird design.
SEE PAGE 46

A simple, yet elegant sofa upholstered in plain blue to complement the blue tones of the drape fabric.
SEE PAGE 72

These cushion covers are subtly coordinated with the drapes without giving the scheme too uniform a look.
SEE PAGE 52

White painted floorboards give a fresh quality and provide a neutral backdrop to the overall decorative scheme.
SEE PAGE 36

The pale and simply decorated rug softens the plain white floorboards.
SEE PAGE 36

Pale greens, blues, and creams were favored colors for the walls in an Arts and Crafts interior.
SEE PAGE 18

The popularity of Morris's Sussex chairs has made them an essential component of an Arts and Crafts interior. Although they are now collectors' items, the basic style and design is still in demand as reproduction furniture.
SEE PAGE 64

DRAPES

Fabric when **folded** and **draped** has a life of its own and Morris's **flowing motifs** based on natural forms suit a **simple** window treatment. Dense brocade patterns such as Iris and Larkspur add a sense of **urban grandeur** to a room, whereas designs such as Honeysuckle or Willow suit the **informality** of a rural cottage. Although the full range of Morris drape fabric designs is no longer available, Sanderson's has the right to print his designs and stocks about 20 patterns. Many commercial outlets can supply the later fabric **designs** of Candace Wheeler, Voysey, and Walter Crane.

William Morris's Peacock and Dragon design, c.1878 shows off his revival of old techniques, including the use of vegetable dyes and block printing methods.

CHOOSING YOUR MATERIAL

Since the nineteenth century – largely as a result of the work of Arts and Crafts designers – cotton chintzes have been regarded as important artworks in their own right rather than as a mere backdrop to the rest of the interior decor.

Morris & Co.'s Jasmine Trail or Jasmine Trellis design. Morris frequently used the trellis motif as a means of structuring the repeats of a design.

Pair of Morris & Co. printed velveteen drapes by J.H. Dearle, c.1890. J.H. Dearle started out in life as Morris's assistant, but became responsible for a considerable amount of the firm's later design work.

Sanderson's Daisy print. Originally a wallpaper design, Daisy works well as a cotton fabric and is particularly suitable for a quiet bedroom or a country sitting room.

Sanderson's Fruit print. One of the main reasons for the success of Morris's chintzes was his use of natural dyes as opposed to the lurid and cheap aniline dyes common in the nineteenth century.

Sanderson's Chrysanthemum print. This simple structure of intertwining stems is brought to life by Morris's passion for natural forms and understanding of how they grow.

Arts and Crafts cotton prints are equally at home in a modern interior as they are in more historical ones. From the second half of the nineteenth century onward, printed cottons replaced the use of heavy velveteens or woven fabrics for drapes. Morris, in particular, loved to explore the textual qualities of cloth and designed numerous patterns using natural fibers and dyes.

Morris & Co.'s Marigold design. Produced by Morris & Co. as a chintz and a wallpaper. Thanks to its neutral color tones, this design is particularly suitable for bathroom or bedroom drapes in conjunction with plain white walls and woodwork.

Sanderson's Bird and Anemone print. Morris produced this design alongside Brer Rabbit and Strawberry Thief. All three designs reveal his romanticized vision of the English countryside.

Sanderson's Bird and Anemone print. As with many of Morris's wallpaper designs, drape fabrics work effectively in different color combinations.

Sanderson's Willow Bough print. Simple and fresh, this is one of Morris's drape designs that can be used in conjunction with the same wallpaper pattern, without creating too heavy an effect.

Sanderson's Compton print. The rich claret, olive, and light-brown color tones of this fabric provide a particularly warm atmosphere to a room when used as a drape fabric.

Sanderson's Honeysuckle print. A complex design in which the delicate, circular honeysuckle blossoms complement the more dominant stylized blooms.

WINDOW TREATMENTS

Avoid elaborate fringes and trimmings and make sure that the fabric suits the decorative scheme of the room. The best way to **display** a Morris or Arts and Crafts fabric is to suspend it on **wooden rings** threaded along a polished wooden or metal **pole**. By the end of the nineteenth century, window treatments became even more **simple**. American Arts and Crafts designers advocated the use of simple **white linen,** cotton, or **translucent**

Candace Wheeler's
"Consider the lilies of the field" drape. An embroidered and painted portière (door drape) created by the American fabric and wallpaper designer Candace Wheeler in 1897.

net. If you have lots of internal pattern work such as wallhangings and brightly colored rugs, **plain cotton** drapes will prove very successful by contrast.

HOW TO RECOGNIZE ARTS AND CRAFTS WINDOW TREATMENTS

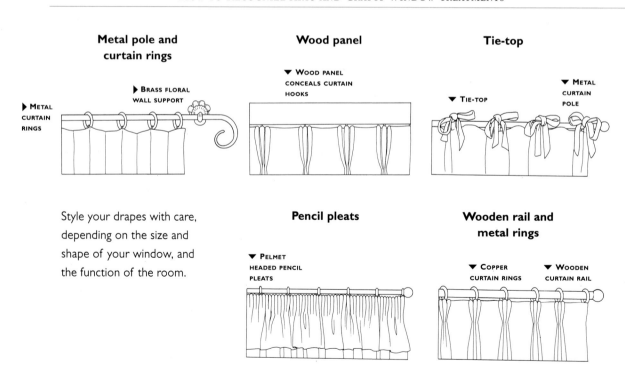

Metal pole and curtain rings

▶ BRASS FLORAL WALL SUPPORT

▶ METAL CURTAIN RINGS

Style your drapes with care, depending on the size and shape of your window, and the function of the room.

Wood panel

▼ WOOD PANEL CONCEALS CURTAIN HOOKS

Tie-top

▼ TIE-TOP

▼ METAL CURTAIN POLE

Pencil pleats

▼ PELMET HEADED PENCIL PLEATS

Wooden rail and metal rings

▼ COPPER CURTAIN RINGS

▼ WOODEN CURTAIN RAIL

Burrows & Co.'s Meadow Lily. This drape works well in any style of home where a simple and lighter lace pattern is required. It is particularly suitable for a bathroom or kitchen, or anywhere where a little privacy is desired.

Burrows & Co.'s The Stag, designed by Voysey. Try and hang the curtain full out so that the design can be displayed to its best advantage.

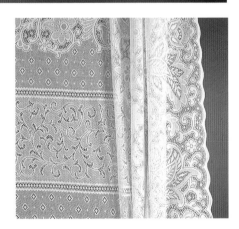

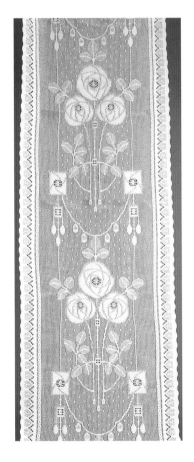

Burrows & Co.'s Kelvin Rose panels. This panel features the famous Glasgow rose which was so integral to the work of Charles Rennie Mackintosh and the Glasgow School. Due to the relatively small scale of the design, it is best applied to a small bathroom or kitchen window.

Burrows & Co.'s Albertine panels. A Scottish design discovered by John Burrows in an English textile archive. These long lace panels are particularly suited to bay windows or the very tall windows of high-ceilinged rooms.

OTHER TEXTILES

The latter part of the nineteenth century witnessed an increased **interest** in textiles, and it was the Arts and Crafts Movement in particular that elevated **textile craft** to a higher art form, improving the status of designers in this field. As a result, textiles of various forms are an **integral** part of the Arts and Crafts interior and can range from sophisticated **woven fabrics**, silk hand-embroidered **cushion covers** and table mats, to the revival of **American** textile techniques.

Even if you are unable to buy an original Arts and Crafts piece, you will find many **modern versions**

Morris's Woodpecker Tapestry. This is one of the very few tapestries designed entirely by Morris. The borders bear the legend, "I once a king and chief, now am the tree-bark's thief, ever twist trunk and leaf, chasing the prey."

HOW TO RECOGNIZE ARTS AND CRAFTS WALLHANGINGS

When you position your wallhanging, make sure sunlight doesn't fall directly on it, as it will fade.

Floral wallhanging

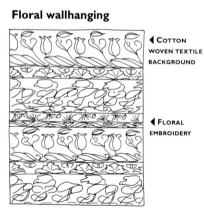

◀ COTTON WOVEN TEXTILE BACKGROUND

◀ FLORAL EMBROIDERY

◀ GEOMETRIC STYLIZATION OF FLORAL MOTIFS

◀ WOVEN COTTON CLOTH BACKGROUND

Stylized floral wallhanging

Leafy wallhanging

▶ ELABORATE CENTRAL PANEL

▶ ACANTHUS LEAF BORDER

Glasgow style wallhanging

▶ DECORATION EMBROIDERED IN SILK

▼ NEEDLEWORK EDGES

Wallhangings have a long history dating back to the tapestries and embroidered cloths traditionally hung in medieval halls. Morris, in particular, had a great enthusiasm for the use of fabric wall coverings and it is somewhat ironic that he, as a great designer of wallpaper, regarded the latter as second best to a hanging.

Embroidered panel (silk on linen), designed for Morris & Co. by J. H. Dearle, c.1885. Morris was particularly influential in reviving traditional methods of weaving and embroidery, and passed on much of his knowledge to his assistant and ultimate successor, J. H. Dearle.

Pomona designed by Edward Burne-Jones, c.1885. Although never a partner of Morris & Co., the painter Burne-Jones provided most of the firm's figurative designs for tapestry and stained glass. Morris designed the floral background and border design.

The linear design of this woven wool hanging is attributed to Ann Macbeth, the successor of Jessie Newberry as teacher of fabric design at the Glasgow School of Art, c.1905.

in the Arts and Crafts style. Look out for **ethnic** textiles and **traditional** style quilts, and hang them on your walls or drape them over your bed. **Quilts** provide a strong dose of **color** and there's no reason why such a piece should not be applied as a wallhanging to **brighten up** plain white walls or wooden paneling. It's amazing how cushions, wallhangings, and **linens** can immediately change the look and feel of a room.

An American quilt such as this one, made in 1888, would complement an Arts and Crafts interior.

OTHER TEXTILES

Whatever use they were put to – cushion covers, bed linen, runners, and chair backs – embroidered, woven, and printed textiles tended to feature floral motifs.

Printed silk designed for the Wiener Werkstätte by Lotte Froemmel-Fochler, 1912. Although the Wiener Werkstätte designers were influenced by the English Arts and Crafts Movement, they were also willing to embrace Modernism.

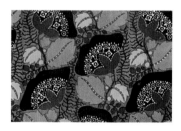

Silver Studio woven silk and cotton, double cloth, 1898. Silver Studio contributed directly to the reputation of British textiles on the Continent and when Liberty & Co. opened, it was Silver Studio textile designs that proved most popular.

Liberty & Co. woven silk panel designed by Arthur Willcock, c.1900. Although Willcock's textile designs display highly original and attractive patterns, his name is little known within the history of textile design.

Alexander Morton linen and chenille panel, c.1900. Like Morris, Morton experimented with natural dyes and fabrics. He founded his highly successful works in Ayrshire, Scotland, along the same principles as Morris & Co.

Alexander Morton double weave silk panel, c.1900. Morton contracted many of the leading Arts and Crafts designers of the day to do textile designs, notably Voysey and Butterfield.

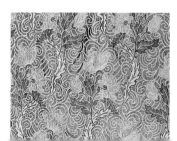

This exquisite Tree of Life embroidered bedspread has a rustic feel traditional to the craft of American needlepoint. Its intricate pattern is best offset by plain walls and textiles.

Jessie Newberry table runner embroidered silk and wool with stylized flower motif. Newberry taught embroidery at the Glasgow School of Art and was influential in introducing the Glasgow style to textile design.

Morris's Apple Tree design embroidered silk on linen, c.1880. Morris and later Arts and Crafts textile designers advocated a much more creative approach to embroidery through a freer translation of designs and the use of natural dyes and fabrics.

Cushion cover with Morris's Trellis design by Beth Russell. Although Morris did not design Trellis to be worked as a cushion cover, it actually proves rather effective for this purpose because the square format of the trellis is in harmony with the square shape of the cushion.

A Glasgow School table runner of embroidered wool on linen with a geometric design attributed to Ann Macbeth. The linear nature of this design is characteristic of the Glasgow style.

LIVING ROOM

Designers in the Arts and Crafts Movement advocated a **bold** and **imaginative** use of **upholstery** fabric as a means of introducing points of **color**. Further-

Leather upholstery is a good option for Arts and Crafts furniture. It is timeless, comfortable, and – if well-treated – lasts for years.

more, colors and **patterns** could be mixed up according to the size of the room and the number of pieces of **furniture** in question. In the case of this open-plan living-dining area, the exuberant and colorful **fabrics** add a decorative **focus** in an interior where there is a lot of exposed **brick** and **woodwork**.

Oak mantel clock,
c.1900, with arched top, exposed bell, brass dial with raised pattern, and brass edging.
SEE PAGE 98

Simple modern reproduction lights hung in traditional "Mackintosh style" as promoted by the Glasgow School of Art.
SEE PAGE 120

Refectory style table with central runner and x-braced legs.
SEE PAGE 76

Ceramics collection from the late eighteenth, nineteenth, and twentieth centuries, with plates, jugs, and vases.
SEE PAGE 112

Oak sideboard,
c.1895, by J.A.S. Schoolbred & Co. Includes mirror with curved stained glass cupboards at either side. The lower cupboard doors feature hand-carved motifs of vine leaves and grapes, and brass handles.
SEE PAGE 86

Liberty-style oak hall chair with solid panel sides, upholstered in fabric, designed by Charles Rennie Mackintosh.
SEE PAGE 64

Orangery fabric by Sanderson's enables the most modern of sofas to fit in with the rest of the room. Here, organic motifs of apples and leaves reflect Arts and Crafts imagery.
SEE PAGE 46

Oak carver armchairs by William Birch with solid curved backs and rush seats.
SEE PAGE 64

UPHOLSTERY

Opt for a **simple** treatment of upholstery fabric, and avoid frills and flounces at all cost. Armchairs and sofas in particular can accommodate a **strong design** both in terms of color and repeats. Simple **Paisley** prints can work well, too, for the upholstery of armchairs or sofas. Alternatively, **geometric designs** can work if the overall interior is relatively plain. Geometric designs became **popular** during the first few years of the twentieth century due to the influence of "New Art" from the European Continent and

Oak armchairs designed by Stanley Webb Davies. Davies's furniture is characterized by his passion for natural materials; he drew links between the furniture we make and the forest trees and animal hides that "gave it birth."

COVERING FURNITURE

Morris used his bold woven designs such as Peacock and Dragon and Briar Rose for the armchairs at Kelmscott Manor (England). Voysey's and Dearle's large fabric designs based on conventional natural forms also worked well for upholstery.

Plain cotton is ideal for upholstery fabric – especially if other fabrics in your room are highly patterned. Choose a rich, earthy color for much-used furniture.

Linen fabric has a wonderful texture and is easy to maintain. Choose a neutral color to complement patterned wallpaper and drapes.

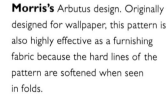

Morris's Jasmine design. Arts and Crafts designers advocated a non-uniform approach to upholstery. You can combine different upholstery fabrics in one room so long as they suit the style of furniture in question.

Morris's Golden Lily design. Morris's fabric designs are particularly effective as upholstery fabrics, even if this was not originally his intended use. Their bold motifs can add an interesting focus to the plain, firm shape of a sofa or armchair.

Morris's Arbutus design. Originally designed for wallpaper, this pattern is also highly effective as a furnishing fabric because the hard lines of the pattern are softened when seen in folds.

The Drawing Room at Standen House, Sussex (England) was designed in 1890 by Philip Webb and furnished with Morris & Co. designs. The reclining chair on the left is upholstered in one of Morris's most popular designs for this purpose, Utrecht Velvet, while the other chair is upholstered in leather with a cushion in Morris's famous Trellis design.

A wing armchair in oak upholstered in Hera Peacock Feather fabric designed by Arthur Silver, c.1900. The Peacock Feather design was made famous by the commercial success of Liberty's from the end of the nineteenth century onward and was applied to a number of mediums apart from upholstery fabric.

William Morris's ebonized chair upholstered in Bird woolen tapestry, c.1870. Bird was woven in wool as a double cloth and consists of alternating pairs of birds, with wings folded and spread, facing and turned away from each other.

Gustav Stickley drew direct inspiration from Morris's reclining chair for this design. However, unlike Morris, Stickley preferred to employ bold designs based on geometric, rather than natural forms, for upholstery fabrics.

the impact of Charles Rennie Mackintosh and the Glasgow School of Art. Geometric designs can also work well to **embellish** Mission-style furniture and were favored by the designer Gustav **Stickley**. If you choose to avoid patterned fabric upholstery, you could try **leather**, which was the favored choice of American designers Greene & Greene, Stickley, and Frank Lloyd Wright. Its **smooth** texture provided a **subtle**

Liberty style. A Kentigern lounge armchair in oak with leather-upholstered sling back designed for Liberty & Co., c.1910.

contrast to their characteristic heavy use of natural woods. **Long plain cushions** can look particularly effective either as a window seat or on a wooden bench.

ALTERNATIVE MATERIALS

Leather, plain rich cotton, linen, or woven fabric can work well as upholstery, especially if offset by carefully chosen cushions. The more worn the leather is – as long as it is well treated – the more beautiful it becomes.

Dark purple leather

Burgundy leather

Rust leather

Brown leather

Dark green leather

Although leather is a highly attractive medium for upholstery, it needs to be kept out of direct sunlight and high levels of light, since it is an organic material and is affected by extremes in temperature and humidity. A leather-upholstered armchair can therefore work well as a corner chair in a library or living room.

Two oak Arts and Crafts chairs from a dining set upholstered in white leather.

An oak wing chair with arm supports and leather upholstered seat and back designed by Ambrose Heal, c.1900.

A Liberty style oak armchair with slatted sides upholstered in original burgundy leather. The design of this chair is attributed to Leonard Wyburd, who was the manager and designer of the store during its formative years.

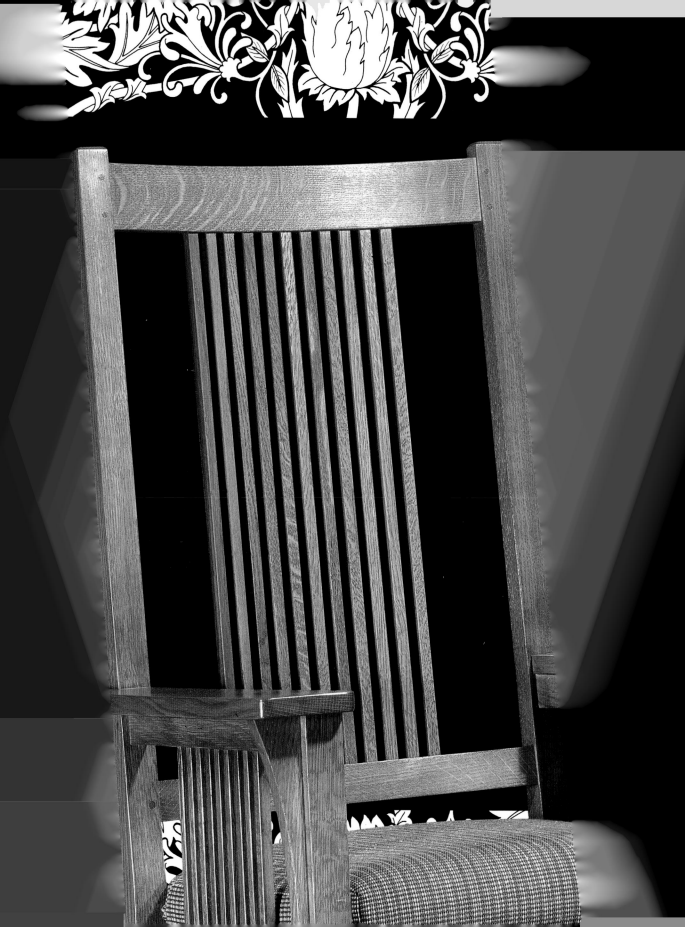

Chapter 3

FURNITURE

Simple designs and honest materials are hallmarks of Arts and Crafts furniture. A wide range including settles, chairs, desks, cabinets, beds, wardrobes, and dressers was made to suit every home. Subsequent furniture designers have added their own distinctive touch.

LIVING ROOM

American Craftsman homes were based on the bedrock virtues of **beauty, simplicity, utility,** and **organic harmony**. Furthermore, their interior designs relied on exposed structural elements, such as **wooden beams** and **stonework,** for decorative details. The latter are enhanced by charming accessories such as these **Stickley**-style reclining armchairs and settles upholstered in a mixture of different but **complementary fabrics.** The drapes are kept simple in keeping with the style of the room.

A Stickley-style armchair is made more comfortable with an upholstered cushion in a pretty eggshell blue.

The high-beamed ceiling, exposed fireplace, white walls, and natural light give this room a spacious, barn-like feel.
SEE PAGE 18

The lattice-backed settle is reminiscent of those marketed in England by Liberty & Co. and Ambrose Heal.
SEE PAGE 72

The Dirk Van Erp lamp, copper tray, and candleholders on the oak topped side table are in keeping with the craft revival style.
SEE PAGE 104

The overall color tones of this room – red drapes, and pink and light green upholstery – are in perfect balance.
SEE PAGE 56

The roughly hewn coffee table has a farmhouse look which adds to the rural feel of this living room.
SEE PAGE 76

The Stickley reclining chairs are in geometric harmony with the ceiling rafters.
SEE PAGE 64

CHAIRS

The simple oak **ladder-back** Sussex chairs designed by Ford Madox Brown provided the prototype for Arts and Crafts dining chairs. Produced by Morris & Co. from 1866, they were relatively **inexpensive.** The most popular design featured a **handcrafted** rush seat and legs connected by a plain stretcher. Gustav Stickley was instrumental in the introduction of Sussex chairs to the United States and his simple Mission dining chair was designed very much along the same lines. Today, **Sussex** and **Mission** chairs have become **sought-after** items. When choosing designs for dining chairs, look for **honest construction,** natural wooden materials, ladder-back or hard-back design, and **finely crafted** rush or leather

Oak chair for the Ingram Street Tea Rooms in Glasgow (Scotland) by Charles Rennie Mackintosh. A number of Mackintosh's chair designs, including this one, are manufactured today by the Italian firm Cassina, who work under a license from Glasgow University.

seating. The Sussex chair was produced in a **variety** of styles: as a corner chair, **armchair**, settle, and round chair and many furniture designers of the Arts and

HOW TO RECOGNIZE ARTS AND CRAFTS CHAIRS

Simple in design and construction, Arts and Crafts chairs are usually made from local hardwoods such as oak with rush or leather seating.

Sussex style

▶ SINGLE RACK OF DECORATIVE SPINDLES

▶ RUSH SEAT

Frank Lloyd Wright chair

▶ DISTINCTIVE VERTICAL SLATS

◀ LEATHER UPHOLSTERY

Glasgow School style

▶ MACKINTOSH-STYLE SQUARE MOTIFS

◀ EBONIZED HIGH CHAIR BACK

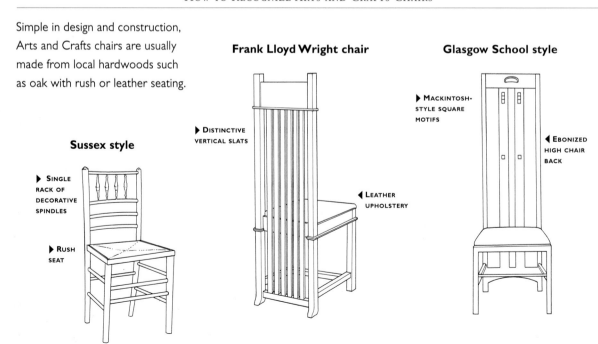

Arts and Crafts architects, notably Frank Lloyd Wright and the Greene brothers, recommended their clients buy Stickley furniture if they weren't able to afford architect-designed originals. The Stickley Manufacturing Co. remains in production in New York State (U.S.A.) to this day.

A pair of oak rush-seated side chairs with heart cut-outs, designed by C.F.A. Voysey. As with many Arts and Crafts furniture designers, Voysey was an architect by training.

Mahogany chair by Ernest Gimson. The demand for light and movable chairs first catered for by Morris & Co. with their Sussex range meant that Gimson's chair-making workshop in Gloucestershire (England) flourished until his death in 1919.

Chair designed by Voysey in 1898. Constructed from oak with a rush drop-in seat, this simple yet highly elegant chair was one of Voysey's favorite designs. He had several in the dining room of his own house in London (England).

Mackintosh Argyll chair designed in 1897 for Glasgow's Argyll Tea Rooms (Scotland). This high-backed oak chair, with its white calico upholstery and a stylized cut-out of a bird in flight in the chair-back, was Mackintosh's first chair design.

Crafts movement created their own version. The famous Morris chair with its adjustable back, ebonized plain wood, and **cushioned seat** and back was the nineteenth-century equivalent to the recliner, designed specifically for its **beauty** and **comfort**. In homage to his English hero, Gustav Stickley made many versions of the Morris chair, although heavier in design and more **simply backed.** Mission chairs influenced other American furniture designers particularly those of the Grand Rapids, U.S.A. Chair designs with a **geometric emphasis** by Charles Rennie Mackintosh and the Austrian Wiener Werkstätte were emulated by G. Charles P. Limbert and Co. of Grand Rapids.

Ambrose Heal Letchworth rush-seated ladder-back armchairs in oak, c.1905. Heal's cottage furniture was designed for the Showcase Housing Exhibition at Letchworth, the first English garden city.

Solid oak chair with heart-shaped cut-out and rush seating, which reveals the consolidation of the work of many Arts and Crafts designers, notably C.F.A. Voysey, Ford Madox Brown, and Ernest Gimson.

OTHER ARTS AND CRAFTS CHAIRS

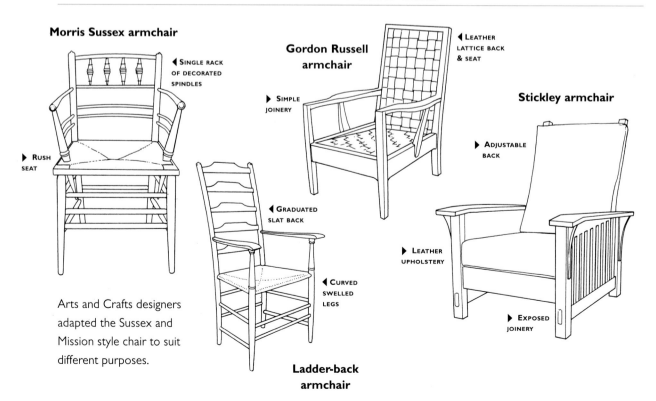

Morris Sussex armchair

◄ SINGLE RACK OF DECORATED SPINDLES

► RUSH SEAT

Arts and Crafts designers adapted the Sussex and Mission style chair to suit different purposes.

Gordon Russell armchair

► SIMPLE JOINERY

◄ LEATHER LATTICE BACK & SEAT

◄ GRADUATED SLAT BACK

◄ CURVED SWELLED LEGS

Ladder-back armchair

Stickley armchair

► ADJUSTABLE BACK

► LEATHER UPHOLSTERY

► EXPOSED JOINERY

Original pieces of Morris furniture – particularly Sussex chairs – can still be found in their various forms. Tones of green are typical to an Arts and Crafts interior.

Liberty & Co. satinwood chair. Liberty's established their own furniture-making workshops in which they used the work of many British designers.

An armchair, probably designed by Ford Madox Brown after traditional chairs from Sussex, England. Very large numbers of these chairs were made and sold very cheaply.

Oak armchair designed by Ernest Gimson in 1903, made in Peter Waals's workshop in 1923. Waals was a Dutch cabinetmaker who came to England in 1900 to work with Gimson, with whom he remained until the latter's death in 1919.

Glasgow School oak barrel armchair with teardrop cut-out motif to inclined back slat, made by Wylie & Lochhead, c.1905. By the 1880s, Wylie & Lochhead employed over 1,700 people to create furniture taken from the designs of the Glasgow School of Art in Scotland.

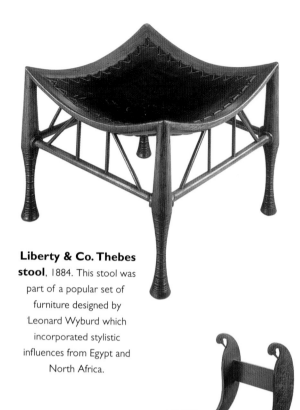

Liberty & Co. Thebes stool, 1884. This stool was part of a popular set of furniture designed by Leonard Wyburd which incorporated stylistic influences from Egypt and North Africa.

A barrel chair in mahogany with upholstered seats and slats extending from arm to sledge base. Attributed to J.S. Henry, c.1900.

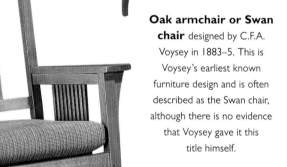

A rocking chair produced from a design by Gustav Stickley. The simple use of oak latticework and the unfussy, yet complementary, upholstered seat are all marks of American Arts and Crafts Mission furniture.

Oak armchair or Swan chair designed by C.F.A. Voysey in 1883–5. This is Voysey's earliest known furniture design and is often described as the Swan chair, although there is no evidence that Voysey gave it this title himself.

Liberty & Co. Wyclif rush-seated chairs in walnut. The strong geometric design of these chairs is attributed to Leonard Wyburd, the first manager of Liberty's.

J. & J. Kohn rocking chair in mahogany-stained beech designed by Gustav Siegel, c.1900. Although German designers were influenced by the English Arts and Crafts advocation of simplicity and fitness for purpose, they rarely executed their own designs, which were made for them by skilled craftsmen using modern machinery.

Extravagant throne chair in walnut with leather seat by G. Fisseux. This flamboyant chair with its imposing Gothic style falls into Morris's second category of furniture, State furniture.

Music armchair in oak with original studded leather seat designed by Richard Riemerschmid, c.1900. Riemerschmid was a highly daring German designer who wholeheartedly embraced the machine. His Maschinenmöbel (reasonably priced machine-made furniture) was enormously popular in Germany.

LIVING ROOM

There is a strong sense of **geometric harmony** in this living room, helped by the lines of the **Mission-style settles** and tables, and the **architectural glass** windows. The simplicity of these furnishings produced by

Gustav Stickley commands a unique sense of **gravitas** appropriate to a living room, which Stickley called "the executive Chamber of the household where the **family** life centers."

William Morris's Sussex settle was based on his original Sussex chair with rushed seat.

Stickley settles are still being made at his old workshop in New York State (U.S.A.).

Pale olive green walls are a common feature of an Arts and Crafts interior.
SEE PAGE 18

The table lamp provides a soft glow and, with its wooden stand and geometric stained glass pattern, is the perfect finishing touch.
SEE PAGE 120

Leather was a popular upholstery material especially among American Arts and Crafts designers.
SEE PAGE 56

The architectural stained glass complements the strong geometry of the Stickley-style furniture.
SEE PAGE 118

Charming accessories such as ceramic vases strategically placed on side tables can help to give a room character.
SEE PAGE 112

The severity of this solid oak Stickley-style settle is offset by the floral pattern of the upholstery, and the soft rug.
SEE PAGE 72

SETTLES

Arts and Crafts designers recommended the **settle** because of its associations with a vanishing rustic past. Settles were a common feature in a **medieval interior** as a means of protection against drafts, the high back giving shelter to the sitter. Line a renovated church pew or a simple **wooden bench** with **cushions** for an Arts and Crafts look. Long wooden benches work well in a **hall** or around a large **oak kitchen table**. For a more comfortable approach choose a simple modern sofa design and carefully **upholster** it in keeping with the rest of the room. Be sure to keep to the **natural shape** of the sofa rather than adding trimmings.

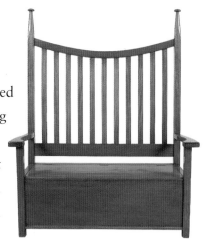

A hall seat in mahogany with high slatted back and blanket box base labeled Liberty & Co., c.1900. This would probably have been designed and marketed for a long hallway.

HOW TO RECOGNIZE ARTS AND CRAFTS SETTLES

The most common settle designs feature a plain oak frame and back furnished with a long upholstered seat cushion.

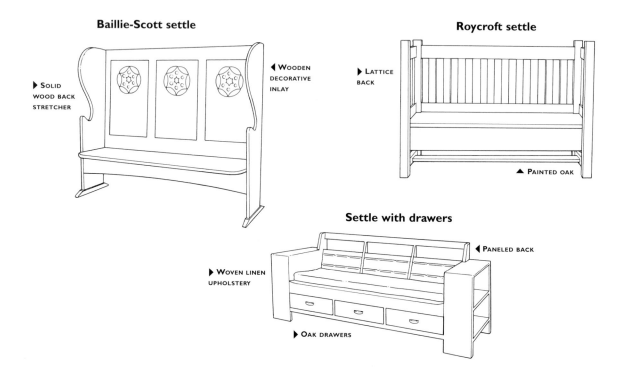

Baillie-Scott settle

◀ SOLID WOOD BACK STRETCHER

◀ WOODEN DECORATIVE INLAY

Roycroft settle

▶ LATTICE BACK

▲ PAINTED OAK

Settle with drawers

▶ WOVEN LINEN UPHOLSTERY

◀ PANELED BACK

▶ OAK DRAWERS

The prototype of the futon sofa bed: an all-oak Stickley settle with a pullout bed beneath. Unstained oak and the simple pattern of the upholstery fabric provide a fine complement to the wood-paneled walls of this interior.

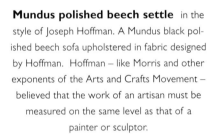

Mundus polished beech settle in the style of Joseph Hoffman. A Mundus black polished beech sofa upholstered in fabric designed by Hoffman. Hoffman – like Morris and other exponents of the Arts and Crafts Movement – believed that the work of an artisan must be measured on the same level as that of a painter or sculptor.

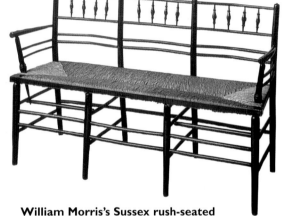

William Morris's Sussex rush-seated settle was as popular as the Sussex chair thanks to its relatively low price and adaptability within an interior.

Oak settle by Sidney Barnsley, c.1919–23. Barnsley designed many versions of the settle with a chamfered lattice back.

LIVING ROOM

Arts and Crafts designers produced tables for **every room** in the house, not just the dining room. Although **occasional tables** are useful in a living room for the **effective** positioning of **table lamps**, metalwork, and other decorative objects, they are only **appropriate** in an Arts and Crafts interior so long as they fulfill their **mission** of usefulness. Therefore, try to avoid cluttering up a room with extraneous **tables** and make sure they are **in keeping** with the rest of the interior.

Modern furniture designers such as Darrell Peart have been influenced by Arts and Crafts craftsmanship and style.

This stenciled border of floral motifs provides a neat demarcation between the wood paneled walls and the plain white-beamed ceiling.
SEE PAGE 32

Stickley based the design for his famous reclining chair on William Morris's prototype.
SEE PAGE 64

Wooden candlesticks enhance the American Craftsman feel of this room.
SEE PAGE 98

This Stickley-style cabinet provides an ideal means of storage for books as well as continuing the geometric theme of the interior.
SEE PAGE 86

Copper lamp bases, complete with a yellow-leaded glass shade, were particular to the American Arts and Crafts Movement.
SEE PAGE 120

Geometric patterns were made popular by Gustav Stickley and Greene & Greene, and are particularly suitable for a Stickley-style settle.
SEE PAGE 72

The pink-red tones of the large rug provide a warm focus in the largely wood-dominated interior.
SEE PAGE 36

TABLES

In the Victorian house, most tables would have been heavily covered in fabrics: the thought of leaving wood **exposed** was completely unacceptable. The message from Arts and Crafts designers was to have only table surfaces that fulfilled a **function**. A simply designed **pine** or **oak** table lacking in ornamental finery enhanced an interior and cut down on clutter. Arts and Crafts furniture designers reacted against the use of heavy mahogany and veneer and advocated **honestly constructed** trestle tables from **native** woods. Their large practical tables are reminiscent of those used in long **medieval dining halls**. A fine dining table surrounded by simple dining chairs provided the **focal point** of a dining room – one of the most important rooms where a family gathered daily.

Mahogany table by Charles Rennie Mackintosh, 1918. The squares of mother-of-pearl inlay on the surface of this table impose a strong graphic element on what is essentially a simple table design.

HOW TO RECOGNIZE ARTS AND CRAFTS TABLES

The Arts and Crafts table is characterized by a simple use of natural, unstained woods – mainly oak, pine, and mahogany.

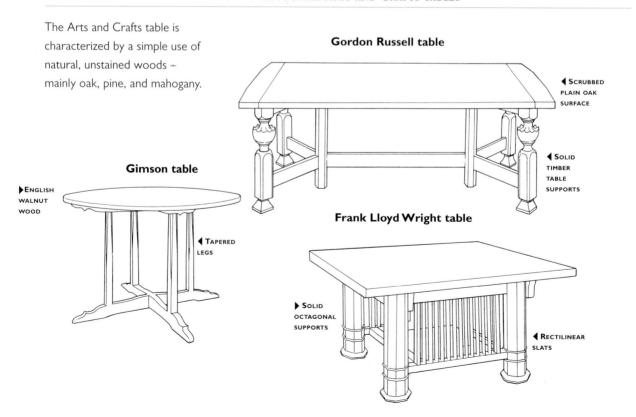

Gordon Russell table

◀ SCRUBBED PLAIN OAK SURFACE

◀ SOLID TIMBER TABLE SUPPORTS

Gimson table

▶ ENGLISH WALNUT WOOD

◀ TAPERED LEGS

Frank Lloyd Wright table

▶ SOLID OCTAGONAL SUPPORTS

◀ RECTILINEAR SLATS

Booth Howell table and four high-backed chairs in oak with metal and leather detail.

Mahogany table by W. R. Lethaby. The wavy line of the table legs set on golden bases gives this table a distinctly Gothic air.

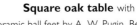

Mission table designed by Stickley, whose furniture became known as the Mission style partly because of his frequently repeated statement that "a chair, a table, a bookcase or bed [must] fill its mission of usefulness as well as it possibly can."

Square oak table with ceramic ball feet by A. W. Pugin. Between 1844 and his death in 1852, Pugin designed over 1,000 pieces of furniture from the study of medieval originals, including 100 tables and 49 armchairs.

Oak side table designed for Morris & Co. by Philip Webb. Morris left Webb in charge of furniture production after Webb built and designed most of the interior for Morris's Red House in Kent (England).

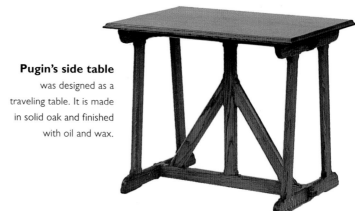

Pugin's side table was designed as a traveling table. It is made in solid oak and finished with oil and wax.

Ambrose Heal & Co. dining table and six chairs in walnut, c.1922. The table has lattice end supports and ebony stringing, and the chairs have lattice backs and ebony dowels, a reflection of Gimson's and Barnsley's influence. Thanks to Heal's espousal of the machine, his furniture designs reached a wider proportion of the market than handcrafted furniture.

Oak Mission dining table. By the beginning of the twentieth century, Mission-style furniture had become highly popular in the United States, to the point that retailers were scarcely able to keep up with the demand.

This Morris pine table is one of the few items of furniture designed by Morris himself and was made for the rooms he shared with the Pre-Raphaelite painter Burne-Jones in London, (England) during the mid-1850s.

Due to its integral role in family life, the dining room must be considered as one of the most important rooms in the house. This impressive Stickley table with the imposing Harvey Ellis chairs provide a ceremonious atmosphere in this dining area.

Table attributed to J.D. Crace, one of Pugin's main collaborators. This octagonal table was possibly a copy of a Pugin design that was originally exhibited at the Medieval Court at the Great Exhibition, London (England) in 1851.

Elaborate oak "Side Table" designed by Bruce J. Talbert, whose furniture is characterized by the use of unstained oak and rich, elaborate moldings based on naturalistic designs.

Contemporary designers are still influenced by the Arts and Crafts style. American designer Darrell Peart was recently inspired by a 1909 Greene & Greene dining table to make this piece.

HOME OFFICE

Arts and Crafts **desks** were built in all shapes and sizes – such as flat-topped, drop-leaf, and rolltop – but all were a perfect marriage of **form and function**. Women's desks were often placed in the main **bedroom**, which doubled up as a sitting room where the lady of the house would retire at certain times of the day to write her **letters** and maybe even a **journal**. Other desks were often located in the **library** – usually the husband's domain. These days, as the line separating the roles of rooms has blurred, desks tend to be found in the **living room** or **home office**.

This walnut writing table with leather top, c.1870, makes an elegant desk for a home office.

Oak dresser with copper strap hinges and mirror is a beautiful and light storage facility. It is also useful for displaying ornaments such as a copper planter with floral motifs.
SEE PAGE **90**

Pewter ornaments such as a Liberty's Tudric biscuit barrel, a Warwick clock, a candlestick, and a box styled after Archibald Knox, unite the elements in the room.
SEE PAGE **104**

An oak occasional table with stylized tulip motifs provides a useful surface for a candle or lamp, a picture frame, and a book.
SEE PAGE **76**

White walls are the perfect backdrop for a room busy with furniture and fabrics. The green-painted dado rail is in keeping with Arts and Crafts interiors.
SEE PAGE **18**

Oak bureau with stylized tulip piercings and drop-leaf front. Once the desk is opened, correspondence can be stored in pigeon-holes, and the flat leaf is an ideal writing surface. Books can be stored on the shelves below.
SEE PAGE **82**

Oak reclining seat upholstered in Morris's Acanthus and Bird fabric design.
SEE PAGE **64**

A pair of rush-seated beech Sussex side chairs provide extra seating in case of visitors.
SEE PAGE **64**

A mahogany flat-topped desk with pigeonholes for storing letters. The flat top may be a more roomy option if you wish to spread your work over an area.
SEE PAGE **82**

DESKS

The earliest supporters of the Arts and Crafts movement tended to be **intellectual** and **artistic,** so the desk was an important **feature** of the home. The American designer Charles Rohlfs produced numerous desk designs from about 1900 onward constructed from **oak** with **carved** decorations. Like other Arts and Crafts furniture these are now out of reach of most people's budgets, but there are many alternative **desk** designs on the market. Choose a simple wood design with a flat **leather** top or one with **pigeonholes** to store your paperwork.

An English walnut writing table made around 1870. Arts and Crafts furniture makers, such as Gimson and Barnsley, were responsible for a revival in walnut, a timber that had fallen out of favor in the early eighteenth century because of the popularity of mahogany.

HOW TO RECOGNIZE ARTS AND CRAFTS DESKS

Natural materials, clean lines, and clever storage make an Arts and Crafts desk a timeless, yet practical choice.

Stickley flat-top desk

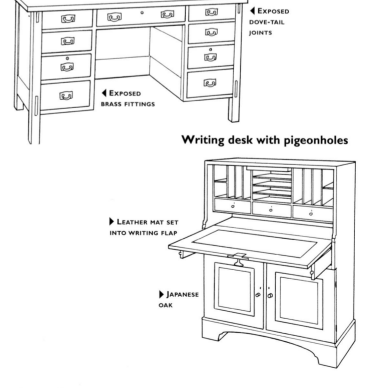

▶ EXPOSED DOVE-TAIL JOINTS

◀ EXPOSED BRASS FITTINGS

Gothic "State" style desk

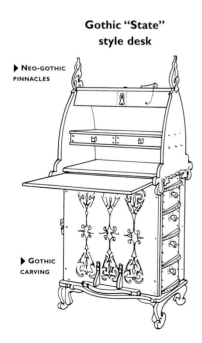

▶ NEO-GOTHIC PINNACLES

▶ GOTHIC CARVING

Writing desk with pigeonholes

▶ LEATHER MAT SET INTO WRITING FLAP

▶ JAPANESE OAK

This modern-day Stickley oak desk and storage unit fulfill a highly practical function, but because of their aesthetic beauty they don't appear too utilitarian.

The lightness yet solidity of this modern desk designed by American furniture-maker Darrell Peart points to Greene & Greene's influence.

Desk for Hill House bedroom in Helensburgh (Scotland) by Charles Rennie Mackintosh, c.1904 (both open and closed). Mackintosh's desks and cabinets tend to be highly decorative with various inlays of mother-of-pearl and colored glass. The interior of this desk is fitted with pigeonholes and a practical, sliding writing surface.

This highly decorative bookcase and desk by R. Norman Shaw combines the grandeur of Morris's State furniture and Pugin's decorative interpretation of Gothic motifs and forms.

Marquetry escritoire and stand, designed by George Jack for Morris & Co., 1893. In 1890 George Jack became chief designer to Morris & Co., and was responsible for many of the quasi-eighteenth-century pieces carried out in mahogany with inlaid decoration.

An oak writing desk designed by Voysey illustrates how solid oak and elaborate metal hinges can give a writing desk a distinct medieval feel equal to that of Voysey's Kelmscott Cabinet (see page 88).

Roycroft writing desk (both open and closed). The Roycroft community was a commercial enterprise and artists' colony founded by Elbert Hubbard in East Aurora, New York State (U.S.A.). Roycroft furniture is characterized by its extreme simplicity and was perhaps the most medieval in appearance of American Arts and Crafts furniture.

Desk by Harvey Ellis.
Ellis briefly joined Stickley's workshop in 1903, where he was influential in adding a touch of grace to the firm's furniture production.

The Jugendstil style was named after *Jugend*, the innovative periodical published in Munich which disseminated new ideas of design based on the Art Nouveau love of sinuous curves and individual craftsmanship.

CABINETS

William Morris acknowledged two categories of furniture: necessary **everyday** furniture, such as chairs and tables; and **State** furniture – cabinets and sideboards "which we have quite as much for beauty's sake as for use." The State cabinets produced by Morris & Co. were **highly decorated** and painted with medieval designs.

This St. George oak cabinet – designed by Philip Webb with painted panels by Burne-Jones – was an attempt to construct the Romantic chests and cabinets depicted in Pre-Raphaelite painting.

However, these furniture pieces were very **expensive** and generally commission-based. Later designers such as Voysey and the craftsmen community in the Cotswolds produced **simple, plain wooden** cabinet designs, often with the hinges and metalwork exposed as a **decorative** feature. Liberty's established their own cabinet-making workshops, which produced simple **country-style** oak dressers. Similarly, American furniture designers favored the solid wooden style as opposed to the ornate, painted cabinets first produced by Morris & Co.

HOW TO RECOGNIZE ARTS AND CRAFTS CABINETS

Cabinets of this period range from the highly ornate example of the late Gothic revival to the simple plain oak designs of American Mission furniture.

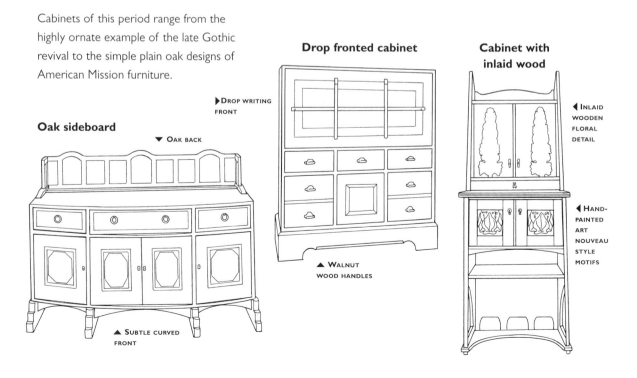

Oak sideboard

▼ OAK BACK

▲ SUBTLE CURVED FRONT

Drop fronted cabinet

▶ DROP WRITING FRONT

▲ WALNUT WOOD HANDLES

Cabinet with inlaid wood

◀ INLAID WOODEN FLORAL DETAIL

◀ HAND-PAINTED ART NOUVEAU STYLE MOTIFS

Marquetry cabinet in walnut, ebony, and holly with whitebeam drawers and silver fittings, designed by Ernest Gimson, 1906. For this design, it is thought that Gimson was inspired by Spanish *bargueño* cabinets and spice cabinets with small drawers typical in the seventeenth century.

Hugh McKay Baillie-Scott display cabinet in oak with checker and pewter inlay, c.1900. Baillie-Scott's numerous furniture designs, over 140 in total, were sold through Liberty's and John White's showrooms in London (England).

Cabinet with painted decoration by Charles Rennie Mackintosh. This display cabinet was designed in 1902 as part of a pair for Mackintosh's own use in his Main Street flat, Glasgow (Scotland). The interior of the cupboard doors is adorned with stylized female figures proffering large rosebuds.

A glazed mahogany cabinet inlaid with brass, ebony, and boxwood, with brass fittings, c.1904. Sinuous curves were the hallmark of Joseph Hoffman's furniture designs for the Secessionist School based in Vienna (Austria).

The sideboard or buffet server was a favorite among Gustav Stickley and his circle, and contained many storage compartments as well as a useful display space within a dining or living room. The handwrought metal handles and hinges give this oak Mission-style piece an appropriately rustic feel, particularly if used to display Arts and Crafts pewter or ceramics.

The Kelmscott Cabinet, designed by Charles Voysey, c.1899. This idiosyncratic oak cabinet was commissioned by Morris to house the original copy of his *Kelmscott Chaucer* published in 1896. The simplicity of the design and wood is set against highly decorative lettering and floral brass fittings.

Wall cabinet with elaborate incised ornament designed by John Moyr Smith and manufactured by Cox & Sons. The latter started out as suppliers of ecclesiastical furniture, later branching out as cabinet carvers and manufacturers of artistic furniture.

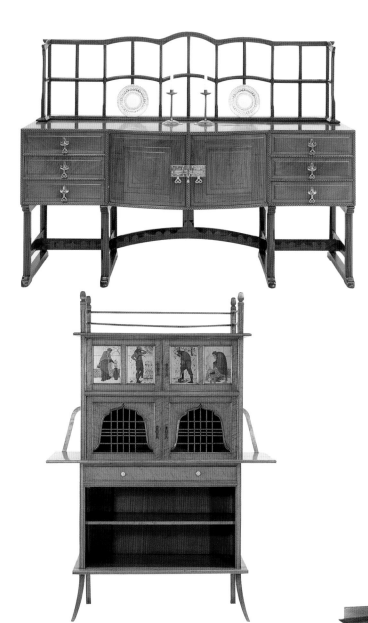

Walnut sideboard with plate stand designed by Ernest Gimson, made by Ernest Smith and Percy Burchett in 1915. Gimson's workshop was very labor-intensive. The plate rack of this sideboard took 453 hours to construct and the metal handles took 98 hours.

Oak sideboard probably designed by George Freeth Roper. Similar to the work of Godwin's later "cottage" furniture, Roper was accused by Godwin of "slavish imitation."

Satinwood cabinet with painted panels, c.1877, designed by E.W. Godwin. Godwin was an early collector of Japanese prints and crafts, which may have influenced the painted panels and delicate wooden struts of this cabinet. His later, simpler, furniture designs were known as "cottage" furniture.

New Studio sideboard in oak with three cupboards and one drawer below leaded-glass doors, all with brass handles, produced for Liberty & Co., c.1898.

KITCHEN DRESSERS

Before the introduction of modern kitchen units, the **dresser** was a stock feature of most kitchens. A **pine** kitchen dresser can create a suitably **rustic** feel and provide useful storage space and a means of displaying **decorative tableware** and **ceramics.** However, dressers do take up a lot of space and are comparatively costly. If you do not have room for a dresser or wooden cabinet, ensure that your kitchen is **simply designed** with a lot of exposed **natural** woodwork, **shelving**, and **racks.** Try to keep the surface area as clear of functional equipment as possible.

Pine kitchen dresser, mid-nineteenth century. Today, well-made pine dressers are often available in less exclusive antique shops.

HOW TO RECOGNIZE ARTS AND CRAFTS DRESSERS

Conceal labor-saving kitchen equipment with wooden cabinets and dressers to create a kitchen based on the Arts and Crafts style.

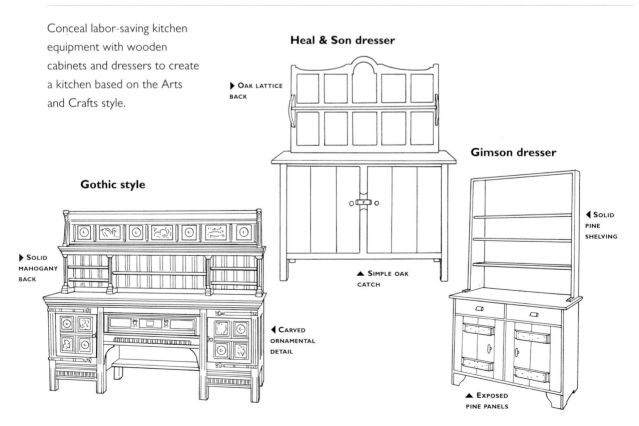

Heal & Son dresser

▶ OAK LATTICE BACK

Gimson dresser

◀ SOLID PINE SHELVING

Gothic style

▶ SOLID MAHOGANY BACK

▲ SIMPLE OAK CATCH

◀ CARVED ORNAMENTAL DETAIL

▲ EXPOSED PINE PANELS

"We believe in having the kitchen small, so that extra steps may be avoided, and fitted with every kind of convenience and comfort, with plenty of shelves and cupboards." (Stickley, 1909).

Hanging Mission wall rack constructed from solid oak, a wall rack is a useful means of displaying prized ceramics and reducing clutter on surfaces.

Stained oak dresser by Ernest Gimson, 1902–5. Initially made for his large country kitchen, Gimson and Barnsley designed many different versions in oak and other less expensive woods.

Oak dresser by W. R. Lethaby, c.1900. The bold dark and light inlays of this dresser are typical of Lethaby's later furniture designs. This design was adapted and popularized by Ambrose Heal.

BEDROOM

Prior to the Arts and Crafts Movement, **bedrooms** were **furnished** and decorated in a similar manner to the drawing or living room, with numerous pieces of furniture and as little **light** as possible. Within the Arts and Crafts home, however, the bedroom was regarded as a **sanctuary** of natural **simplicity** with a light decorative scheme and essential furniture only. This solid **Stickley-style bed** and chest of drawers are skillfully crafted from oak, and they are offset by plain white walls and **minimal** decoration.

This oak wardrobe by Barnsley looks deceptively simple. but the skill involved in the curve of the front was immense.

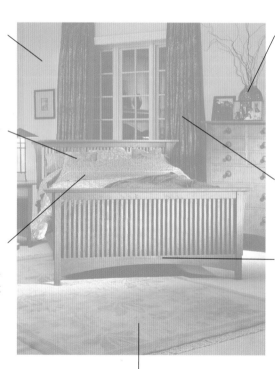

For the first time, plain white walls became completely acceptable within an interior.
SEE PAGE 18

The cushions scattered across the bed are upholstered in Morris's Acanthus design, produced in a red pattern.
SEE PAGE 52

The bedlinen produced from Morris's fabric designs provides a decorative focus among the plain woodwork and white walls.
SEE PAGE 52

Simple metal accessories, such as the bedside lamp on the side table, and the pot and vase on the chest of drawers, add to the rustic feel of this bedroom.
SEE PAGE 120

Morris's Wandle design works well as a fabric for drapes.
SEE PAGE 46

Suites of wooden bedroom furniture were popular with Arts and Crafts designers. This bedroom features a wooden bed frame with a complementary chest of drawers and bedside cabinet.
SEE PAGE 94

Soft rugs on the bedroom floor will soften the coldest stone, tile, or wooden flooring. Sisal rugs and rush matting were also popular at the time.
SEE PAGE 36

BEDROOM FURNITURE

On the whole, Arts and Crafts bedrooms were furnished simply and designed as **havens** of uncluttered tranquility. William Morris advised low-key decorative schemes for bedrooms, with simple wooden furniture, plain walls, and lots of **natural light**. American and British craftsmen produced a range of beds constructed from solid wood but today it is often more practical to adapt wooden or brass bedsteads to a contemporary **bed frame**. Choose a simply designed wooden wardrobe and chest of drawers. **Willow wicker** furnishings can offer a suitably light feel to a bedroom and are a less expensive option than heavy wooden pieces. And **white-painted** furniture can have a soothing effect. Whatever style of furniture you select, avoid anything that is not essential.

Harvey Ellis night stand.
Constructed from solid oak with handwrought copper handles for the two small drawers. Ellis's designs tend to be lighter and more delicate than his colleague Stickley's.

HOW TO RECOGNIZE ARTS AND CRAFTS BEDROOM FURNITURE

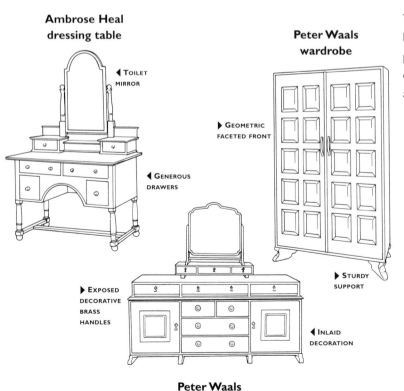

Ambrose Heal dressing table

◀ TOILET MIRROR

◀ GENEROUS DRAWERS

▶ EXPOSED DECORATIVE BRASS HANDLES

Peter Waals dressing table

▶ INLAID DECORATION

Peter Waals wardrobe

▶ GEOMETRIC FACETED FRONT

▶ STURDY SUPPORT

Try to restrict bedroom furniture to a bare minimum. You don't need to purchase a whole bedroom suite, but do try and choose furniture designs and colors that are complementary.

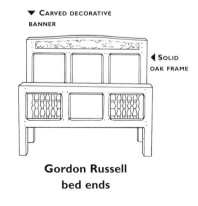

▼ CARVED DECORATIVE BANNER

◀ SOLID OAK FRAME

Gordon Russell bed ends

This beautiful Arts and Crafts oak wardrobe is inlaid with heart-shaped Ruskin enamels, stylized lily fruitwood panels, and features cruciform ring handles.

Oak wardrobe from the Moreton bedroom suite retailed by Liberty & Co. The simple geometric nature of this design works well in a small bedroom or dressing room.

An eccentric chestnut wood wardrobe designed by Ambrose Heal around 1904. The owl design is a throwback to the idiosyncratic use of animal forms of earlier Arts and Crafts designers, notably William de Morgan and Walter Crane.

Athelstan bedroom suite designed for Liberty & Co. around 1909, comprising a wash-stand with dark-green inset tiles and a chest of drawers and mirror – all with heart cut-out motifs.

An ambitious oak wardrobe from Barnsley's Gloucestershire workshops. The curved design of the wardrobe front is unusual and must have involved considerable skill.

The Prioress's Tale wardrobe was designed by Philip Webb in 1859 for William Morris's Red House in Kent (England). It was painted with a Chaucerian theme by the Pre-Raphaelite painter Edward Burne-Jones.

Glasgow School oak wardrobe with inlaid panels of floral motifs in various woods by Wylie & Lochhead, c.1905. By 1905, the furniture produced by Wylie & Lochhead had become a household name throughout Scotland and England.

Three-door wardrobe with Glasgow rose motifs inlaid in copper, abalone, and various woods. Design attributed to George Logan and made by Wylie & Lochhead, c.1900. Like Charles Rennie Mackintosh, an inlaid copper rose motif was the hallmark of Logan's furniture designs.

In Morris's bedroom at Kelmscott Manor, Gloucestershire (England), the valance – embroidered by Jane and May Morris – illustrates a poem by Morris which celebrates the natural beauty of the Gloucestershire country-side he loved.

This Harvey Ellis style Mission bed with inlay is still available from the Stickley workshops in New York State (U.S.A).

Stickley bedpost and panel bed with leather. This post and panel bed is based on a Gustav Stickley design, although it is now larger and taller than the original. The headboard panels are also available in solid wood.

MISCELLANY

Although the **Arts and Crafts** Movement decried the cluttered appearance of Victorian interiors, there is no doubt that the addition of miscellaneous pieces such as an **imposing** grandfather clock, sleek umbrella **stand**, discreet magazine rack, or handcrafted wooden **coffer** can beautify a room and add an idiosyncratic touch. Search in antique stores and contact suppliers for unusual objects that will give you great **pleasure** and also provide a talking point for your guests. These objects are **practical** too, which means that your home won't be overrun by useless knick knacks.

Glasgow School umbrella stand in oak with cut-out handhold to the back and brass uprights. Designed by George Walton, c.1900.

Mission style tall case clock.

HOW TO RECOGNIZE ARTS AND CRAFTS DESIGNS

Look out for common motifs like cut-out hearts and the use of natural materials such as wood and copper.

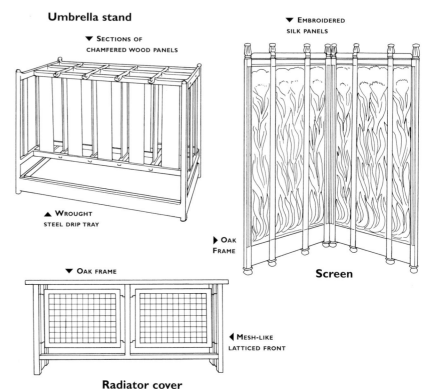

Umbrella stand

▼ SECTIONS OF CHAMFERED WOOD PANELS

▲ WROUGHT STEEL DRIP TRAY

▼ EMBROIDERED SILK PANELS

▶ OAK FRAME

Screen

Box with inlaid wood

▶ EBONY INLAY

◀ WALNUT WOOD

▼ OAK FRAME

◀ MESH-LIKE LATTICED FRONT

Radiator cover

An imposing entry is one of the characteristic spaces of the Arts and Crafts house. The impressive nature of this hallway is enhanced by the magnificent gong and the beautiful yet simple wooden and copper umbrella stand.

Roycroft magazine/book pedestal.

Oak coffer with bronze strapwork hinges extending from top to full length of back. Retailed at Liberty's, the coffer was made by Mrs. Alfred Waterhouse's Yattendon Metalworking Class (created to give occupation to the men in her village in the evening). The class disbanded in 1914 at the outbreak of World War One.

Glasgow School magazine rack in mahogany with round cut-outs to the back and boxwood stringing, c.1905.

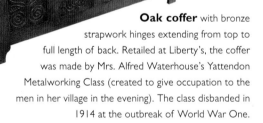

Valkyrie upright grand piano in oak with pewter- and ebony-inlaid stylized flower motif, and steel strap hinges and feet. Designed by L. and F. Wyburd and made by J.J. Hopkinson for Liberty & Co., c.1902.

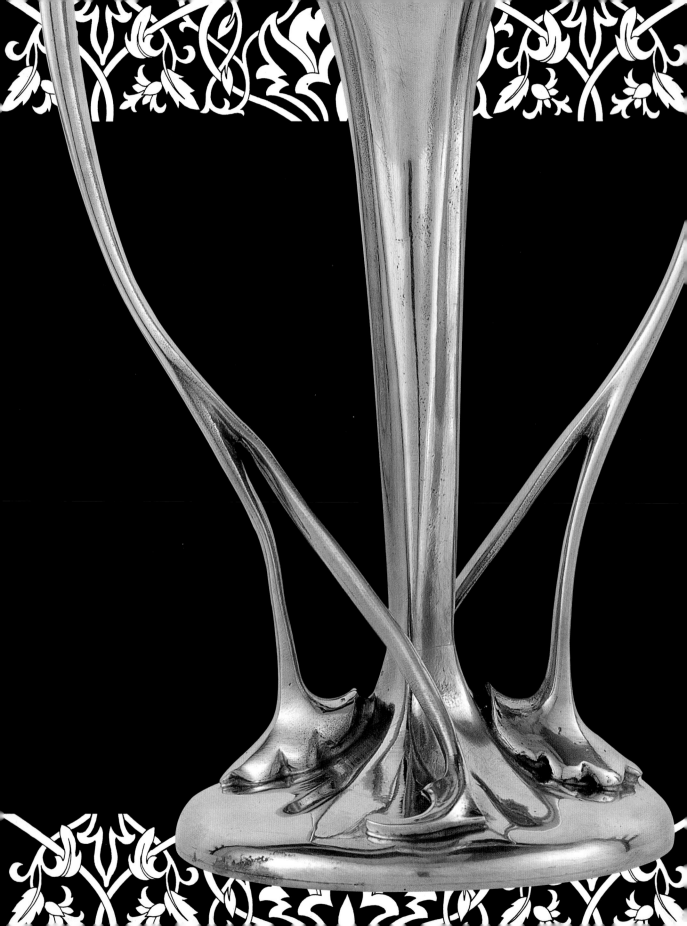

Chapter **4**

ORNAMENTS Numerous small

workshops were set up in America and Europe to

create the metalware, ceramics, and glassware that

are such a joy to collect today. As well as providing

job satisfaction for workers, workshops kept craft

skills alive in the face of booming mass production.

HOME OFFICE

Hand-forged Arts and Crafts metalware was used as hardware in houses and on furniture, particularly simple **copper** and **pewter** that featured **hammer dents**. Copper accessories by Dirk Van Erp are an attractive and practical addition to this **fireplace** in a New York State farmhouse. The fireplace was often the **center** of attention in a living or drawing room – especially in winter – and the metalware, original pine **woodwork**, and exposed **brickwork** make this one particularly welcoming.

Wrought-steel candelabra designed by Ernest Gimson, c.1905.

The Stickley lanterns with heart cut-outs complement the metal plate, box and vase on the mantel.
SEE PAGE 120

A drop-leaf writing desk was an important feature of the Arts and Crafts home and – given the growing tendency to work from home – it is worth creating an aesthetically pleasing workspace for yourself.
SEE PAGE 82

A warming oven to the left of the fireplace is covered by a cast-iron plate.
SEE PAGE 104

The handwrought copper fireplace accessories by Dirk Van Erp include a screen, iron, and fireplace tools.
SEE PAGE 104

Plain walls, exposed timbers and brickwork provide a perfect backdrop for this charming, American Craftsman-style home office.
SEE PAGE 18

A leather-upholstered Stickley armchair and footstool provide a comfortable corner in which to relax.
SEE PAGE 56

Wooden flooring was a common feature of an Arts and Crafts home. Here, the floorboards have been covered by a drugget rug like the ones that Stickley imported from India.
SEE PAGE 36

METALWARE

Arts and Crafts metalware, distinguished by the marks of the hammer and subsequent **rustic** appearance, was first made popular in England by the metalworkers of C.R. Ashbee's Guild of Handicraft. **Simply designed** metalware soon became an essential component of the Arts and Crafts interior, largely due to the commercial **success** of retailers such as Liberty's and to the low cost and **workability** of metal. Metalware was also highly popular in America, where Stickley and Roycroft both had extensive metalworking operations.

A picture frame in pewter with repoussé-work owl and stylized flower motifs. Thought to have been designed by Frank Bazeley, c.1904.

HOW TO RECOGNIZE ARTS AND CRAFTS METALWARE

Many designers created a wide range of metalwork that incorporated decorative motifs such as animals and foliage.

Teapot
◀ BRASS HANDLE & FEET
▶ BEATEN COPPER

Plate
◀ PICTORIAL EMPHASIS
▶ EMBOSSED SILVER DECORATION

Coffee pot
◀ GREEN GLASS TOP
◀ PLAIN SILVER

Dish and cover
▼ LOOPED WIRE HANDLE
▶ ELEGANT LINES

Pitcher
▶ REPOUSSÉ DECORATION
◀ HAMMERED SILVER

Vase
◀ NATURALISTIC SILVER RELIEF
▲ RECTILINEAR VASE FORM

Like most original Arts and Crafts metalware, Heintz art metal vases are now collectors' items. Simple vase designs worked in bronze with an Arts and Crafts silver overlay floral design are the hallmarks of the Heintz style.

Mackintosh clock designed around 1900. Today, interest in Charles Rennie Mackintosh's fittings and fixtures is considerable and many of his designs are in current production.

Liberty Heritage Pewter A design from the famous Tudric collection designed by Archibald Knox in 1902. The hallmarks of Liberty Tudric designs were the decorative Celtic forms and floral motifs which were widely admired and imitated.

Candlestick designed by Philip Webb for Burne-Jones, 1861. Webb appreciated both grandeur and simplicity in his metalware. He made the distinction between daily objects, which should be strong but not overly ornamented, and objects for beauty's sake alone.

Silver and enamel biscuit box designed by Archibald Knox in 1901. Highly practical, yet decorative, with Celtic floral motifs, mother-of-pearl and enamel insets.

Silver, brass, and copper jug by Louis Comfort Tiffany, New York (U.S.A.), c.1900. Although Tiffany is best known for his opalescent glassware, his designs were also adapted to other materials.

Pair of wrought-steel candelabra designed by Ernest Gimson, c.1905. As well as architecture and furniture, Gimson produced designs for leadwork, embroidery, pierced and chased metalwork.

Silver trinket box adorned with Celtic motifs in green enamel, designed by Archibald Knox in 1905 for Liberty's popular Cymric range.

Electroplated two-handled bowl with hinged cover by Christopher Dresser. His sparse tableware designs created from sheet metal inspired the Wiener Werkstätte and pointed to the later Industrial Aesthetic movement

A carved gilt-framed mirror designed by Dagobert Peche with a Wiener Werkstätte paper label, exhibited in the Austrian pavilion at the Paris Exhibition of 1925.

Chased and pierced brass wall sconce designed by Ernest Gimson, c.1905. Gimson set up his own smithy in Gloucestershire (England), where he produced numerous articles of metalware – such as door furniture and light fittings – in brass, polished steel, and iron.

The hand-hammered appearance of this pewter clock case by Liberty & Co. has a rustic look, which foreshadows Knox's later Tudric designs.

Metalware accessories like this lamp, vase, and box will add character and style to your writing desk. Complete the look with some old books from the Arts and Crafts era.

A Liberty Tudric pewter owl jug with inset seashell eyes taken from a design by C.H. Brannam, c.1902. Although Tudric pewter was almost entirely machine-made, at first glance it has the appearance of being handwrought.

Silver-mounted green glass decanter with maker's mark for the Guild of Handicraft, 1901. This guild, founded by Charles Robert Ashbee, first made handbeaten or hammered metalware popular, but the project did not survive because of Ashbee's antipathy to machine production and commerce.

Liberty & Co. rose bowl with Celtic strapwork decoration, 1908. Liberty launched its Cymric silver range alongside Tudric pewter. Although it was largely machine-made, it was finished with a touch of "honest hammering."

Pair of candlesticks by R.L. Llewellyn Rathbone, 1902. Features beaten copper with bands of punched floral ornament. Rathbone had a wide knowledge of metalworking techniques, which he taught at Liverpool University and the London Technical Institute (England).

Brass teapot by Voysey, 1896. The simplicity of this teapot harks back to the Middle Ages. Although Voysey trained as an architect, no aspect of an interior – from fire-tongs to kettle – was too small to win his attention.

Liberty copper repoussé oval mirror, c.1905, features large inset turquoise Ruskin enamel ornaments. The **rectangular mirror**, c.1900, has stylized flower motifs and two inset Ruskin enamel ornaments. **Wall sconces**, c.1900, have a fish and shell motif. Liberty's competitive prices enabled professional firms' designs to reach a wide public – even providing a name, *stile Liberty*, as an alternative to the style more generally known as Art Nouveau.

DINING ROOM

The Victorian **dining table** was an ornate affair, with elaborate linens, crockery, and cutlery. The Arts and Crafts Movement advocated a

Glass goblet designed by James Powell, c.1905. Arts and Crafts glassware and ceramics were less elaborate than their Victorian counterparts, and their beauty came from the skillful crafting of the material itself.

simpler approach based around a number of beautifully designed accessories such as this **Rockwood dinnerware**. The **buffet server** became a typical feature of an Arts and Crafts dining room, as it not only fulfilled a **practical** function – providing a surface from which to serve food – but it was also a means of **displaying** ceramics and metalware.

The buffet server was an integral feature of the Arts and Crafts dining area and proved an effective way to display ceramics and metalware.
SEE PAGE 86

Simple table mats and runners on an undressed table are more typical of an Arts and Crafts dining room than fine, delicate white linens or silks.
SEE PAGE 50

A studded band – often known as the Shreve Strap – distinguishes Shreve & Company's Gothic-inspired silverware cutlery.
SEE PAGE 104

Mica shades with copper hardware were favored by Arts and Crafts designers for lamps, because they offered an indirect and soft light, creating a tranquil ambience.
SEE PAGE 120

Luster glaze ceramic ware was popularized by designers of the Arts and Crafts Movement.
SEE PAGE 112

Rockwood dinnerware provided a simple alternative to the overly ornate ceramics of the Victorian era.
SEE PAGE 112

CERAMICS & GLASS

Art pottery became a phenomenal **success** in Britain largely due to the work of William de Morgan, who produced a wide range of ceramics decorated with **floral** forms. He was also inspired by **Islamic** designs. Other British potteries of renown were the Martin Brothers, Della Robbia, and Moorcroft. As with de Morgan, their motifs were principally floral and leafy with exceptional **luster glazes.** These potteries were aided by the enormous **commercial** success of Liberty's as a retailer through

Tall-necked vase decorated in the Persian manner, 1912; **high-shouldered vase** decorated with panels of dog rose, 1903; both by Richard Joyce.

Galleon vase with heraldic devices by William S. Mycock, 1914. The Pilkington Tile and Pottery Co. was primarily a glassworks until 1897, after which they also produced Royal Lancastrian luster-ware.

HOW TO RECOGNIZE ARTS AND CRAFTS CERAMICS

Look out for art pottery with Islamic influences and luster glazes. Common ceramics motifs include flowers, leaves, and animals.

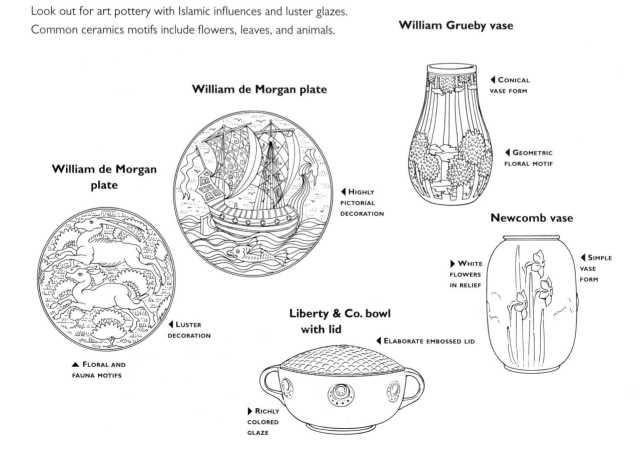

William Grueby vase

◄ CONICAL VASE FORM

◄ GEOMETRIC FLORAL MOTIF

William de Morgan plate

◄ HIGHLY PICTORIAL DECORATION

William de Morgan plate

◄ LUSTER DECORATION

▲ FLORAL AND FAUNA MOTIFS

Newcomb vase

► WHITE FLOWERS IN RELIEF

◄ SIMPLE VASE FORM

Liberty & Co. bowl with lid

◄ ELABORATE EMBOSSED LID

► RICHLY COLORED GLAZE

Arts and Crafts matte glazed pottery was admired for its restrained use of natural motifs and earthy colors.

A painted and glazed vase with flower motif by P. Revere, Boston (U.S.A.), c.1910.

Water jugs in the form of a comical owl, pelican, and heron by Brannan. The decorative use of animal forms was a characteristic of the Arts and Crafts designers.

The Upchurch Potters in England sold their wares through Liberty & Co. This pottery is characterized by a minimum amount of surface decoration and strong shapes. Colors were mostly monochrome and the designs were inspired by Roman prototypes.

William de Morgan plate. De Morgan "rediscovered" the lost art of luster decoration for pottery. Although he is now best known for his tiles, he produced ceramic tableware which is characterized by its boldness of design and strong use of colors.

A 25-piece tea set by Foley Peacock Pottery with stylized Glasgow rose motif, comprising six cups, saucers, and biscuit plate, a sandwich plate, milk jug, cream jug, sugar bowl and cover, and slops dish, designed by George Logan in 1903.

Goblet designed by James Powell, c.1905. Powell's of Whitefriars, London (England) was one of the most prestigious glassworks of the nineteenth century. They provided colored glass for the production of stained glass by Morris & Co.

Tiffany cameo vases Tiffany located his glass factory in Corona, Queens (U.S.A.) in 1893. Thanks to the success of his glassware, he soon had over 300 workers, designers, artists, and glass-blowers at the works.

Loetz gold glass vase c.1900 covered with multicolored iridescence and applied purple spot and stripe decoration, also a Loetz purple iridescent **bowl** to the Austrian Secessionist Kolomon Moser.

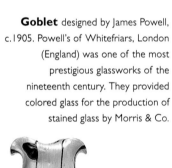

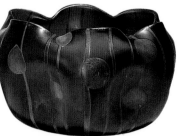

which they sold their wares. Art pottery became enormously **popular** in America with the foundation of such companies as the Chelsea Keramic Art Works at Boston, which developed a number of **sumptuous glazes.** The Rockwood Pottery and ceramicist William Grueby perfected a variety of colors and wares which became widely accessible.

Louis Comfort Tiffany dominated the production of **decorative** glass in America and developed a number of glassmaking techniques, inspired by his own expertise and knowledge of **Roman** and **Middle Eastern** glass, such as **millefiori** and luster. In 1893, he registered his Favrile (meaning **handmade**) trade-

Charger decorated with a ship by the Della Robbia Pottery, Birkenhead (England). Their art pottery, made in emulation of Italian prototypes, proved enormously influential largely thanks to the fact that it was stocked by Liberty & Co.

Blue and gold Favrile "Jack in the Pulpit" glass vase, 1915 by Louis Comfort Tiffany (U.S.A.) .

mark, which went on sale three years later with enormous commercial success. Although Tiffany also produced ceramics, it is his **irides-cent** glass vases and lamps that are now his main legacy.

HOW TO RECOGNIZE ARTS AND CRAFTS GLASS

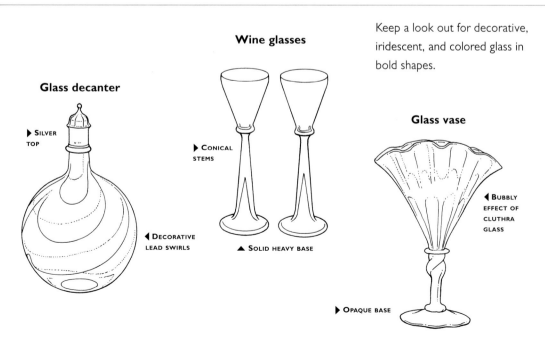

Wine glasses

Keep a look out for decorative, iridescent, and colored glass in bold shapes.

Glass decanter

▶ SILVER TOP

◀ DECORATIVE LEAD SWIRLS

▶ CONICAL STEMS

▲ SOLID HEAVY BASE

Glass vase

◀ BUBBLY EFFECT OF CLUTHRA GLASS

▶ OPAQUE BASE

DINING ROOM

American Arts and Crafts architect and designer Frank Lloyd Wright adopted a **geometric** approach to stained glass design, which was **integral** to his architecture at the time. In this dining room at Willits House, built in 1902 in Illinois, there is a strong sense of **harmony** based on the skillful interplay between the **horizontal** and **vertical** lines of the windows, furniture, and the **structure** of the room itself, which gives it a formal, ceremonial feel.

Flora and fauna motifs were also popular for stained glass, and modern designs have carried on the tradition.

Geometric stained glass in the ceiling and windows of this dining room allow light to fall in golden pools on the floor and table. Frank Lloyd Wright was revolutionary in choosing a geometric pattern for his stained glass.
SEE PAGE 118

Dark green painted walls add a classic touch to the room, relieved by the wooden paneling fitted on the walls. White paint has been used above the window and dado rail, which lightens the whole atmosphere.
SEE PAGE 19

Wall lamps spread a subtle light over the room. The need for overhead lighting is stunningly fulfilled by the stained glass windows in the ceiling.
SEE PAGE 120

A built-in cabinet suits the clean lines of the room and, with its own special lighting, is a perfect display case for prized ornaments, ceramics, and metalware.
SEE PAGE 86

Frank Lloyd Wright oak dining chair, c.1903, designed to complement the scheme of the Willits House dining room. When used around the dining table, these high-backed chairs create the effect of a room within a room.
SEE PAGE 64

Wooden flooring provides the finishing touch to a room that is grand, yet warm and airy.
SEE PAGE 36

Frank Lloyd Wright oak dining table, c.1903, designed as part of a set with oak high-backed chairs.
SEE PAGE 76

STAINED GLASS

An ornamental stained glass window with floral motif shows that, sometimes, less is more.

STAINED GLASS The revival during the nineteenth century of the **medieval art** of stained glass was partly caused by a spate of ecclesiastical building. Morris & Co. was instrumental in introducing stained glass into the home, using clear glass with **painted detail** in paler tones. Through the pioneering work of designers such as Henry Holiday and Christopher Wall, stained glass was used not only in **windows**, but also inset into **doors** and **furniture**. Stained glass was also extremely popular in America. Louis Comfort Tiffany and John La Farge employed layers of **translucent** glass adorned with **rich designs** of flowers, exotic birds, and stylized motifs. Later designers such as Charles Rennie Mackintosh and Frank Lloyd Wright used colored glass, generally unpainted, to create **geometric designs** as part of their decorative schemes.

HOW TO RECOGNIZE ARTS AND CRAFTS STAINED GLASS

Flora and fauna, and geometric designs feature heavily in Arts and Crafts stained glass.

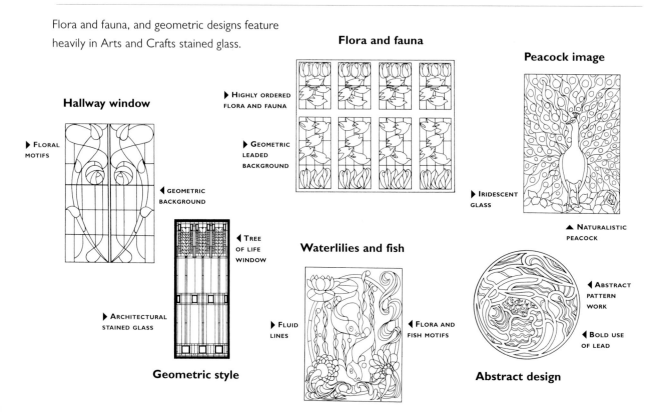

Hallway window

▶ FLORAL MOTIFS

◀ GEOMETRIC BACKGROUND

◀ TREE OF LIFE WINDOW

▶ ARCHITECTURAL STAINED GLASS

Geometric style

Flora and fauna

▶ HIGHLY ORDERED FLORA AND FAUNA

▶ GEOMETRIC LEADED BACKGROUND

Waterlilies and fish

▶ FLUID LINES

◀ FLORA AND FISH MOTIFS

Peacock image

▶ IRIDESCENT GLASS

▲ NATURALISTIC PEACOCK

◀ ABSTRACT PATTERN WORK

◀ BOLD USE OF LEAD

Abstract design

Briar Rose A modern design using common Arts and Crafts motifs of flora and fauna.

"Spring" illustration for Morris's *The Earthly Paradise* by Charles E. Kempe. By the end of the nineteenth century painted glass had become a regular domestic feature. This design was for Wightwick Manor in Staffordshire (England).

Modern stained glass designers can produce beautiful results that reflect the Arts and Crafts style, as shown in this bakery window with its harvesting theme.

Dorigen roundel designed by Edward Burne-Jones and set in a background of floral quarried tiles designed by Morris and Co., c.1876. Morris & Co. gained their initial commercial success through the revival of medieval stained-glass techniques. Whereas Burne-Jones provided most of the designs, Morris was concerned with technique and color.

LIGHTING

The invention of the **light bulb** by Edison in 1879 opened up new possibilities for designers as it allowed them to dispense with oil reservoirs, gas pipes, and the hazards of naked flames. W.A.S. Benson designed numerous lamps, including **glazed pottery** ones inset with **glass**, and **copper** chandeliers. In America, **natural forms** such as flowers inspired lamp design, as the stems could disguise wires and the petals hide light bulbs. Tiffany lamps **glowed** romantically in dark corners, and Stickley and the Roycroft shops produced plain **wooden** lamps in keeping with the Craftsman style.

Suspended light designed by Frank Lloyd Wright for Dana-Thomas House, Illinois (U.S.A.) in 1902. It's thought that Lloyd Wright was inspired by butterfly wings.

Tiffany's leaded-glass lampshades can add a romantic warmth to dark corners of a room, because – unlike spotlights – they diffuse the light in a uniform manner.

HOW TO RECOGNIZE ARTS AND CRAFTS LAMPS

Lighting should be subtle and bring out a room's color scheme. Try and use corner and table lamps as opposed to a strong overhead light.

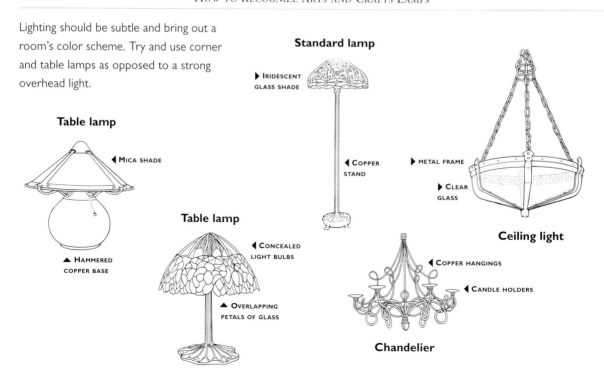

Table lamp

◄ MICA SHADE

▲ HAMMERED COPPER BASE

Table lamp

◄ CONCEALED LIGHT BULBS

▲ OVERLAPPING PETALS OF GLASS

Standard lamp

▶ IRIDESCENT GLASS SHADE

◄ COPPER STAND

▶ METAL FRAME

▶ CLEAR GLASS

Ceiling light

◄ COPPER HANGINGS

◄ CANDLE HOLDERS

Chandelier

The yellow mica shade of this standard lamp offer a glowing light appropriate to the intimacy of the Arts and Crafts interior.

Tiffany Studios 10-light lily pad table lamp with assorted iridescent glass shades, c.1900. Natural forms, especially flowers, were used by Tiffany to disguise the functional elements of lighting. In this case, the stems hide the wiring and the drooping petals conceal the lightbulbs.

Table lamp inspired by the clean lines and simple design of American Arts and Crafts designers. Arroyo products are finished by hand, so no two look exactly alike.

A pair of copper and enamel electric light brackets designed by Charles Robert Ashbee, c.1895. Ashbee's beaten or hammered metalwork was a very popular material for lighting as it provided an interesting surface from which the light could be deflected within a room.

Arroyo Craftsman takes inspiration from the art glass of Frank Lloyd Wright and the natural materials used by Stickley, and Greene & Greene. This ceiling light features gold and white iridescent glass and an antique copper finish.

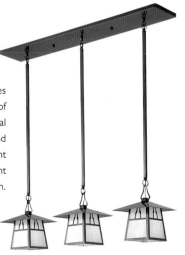

SUPPLIERS

Antiques

Circa 1910 Antiques
7206 Melrose Avenue
Los Angeles, CA 90046
(323) 965-1910

Craftsman Antiques
5701 Telegraph Avenue
Oakland, CA 94609
(510) 595-7977

The Craftsman Home
3048 Claremont Avenue
Berkeley, CA 94705
(510) 655-6503

Fedde's
2350 East Colorado Boulevard
Pasadena, CA 91107
(626) 796-7103

Geoffrey Diner Gallery Inc.
1730 21st Street NW
Washington, DC 20009
(202) 483-5005

Historic Lighting
114 East Lemon Avenue
Monrovia, CA 91016
(626) 303-4899

Michael Fitzsimmons Decorative Arts
311 West Superior Street
Chicago, IL 60610
(312) 787-0496

Peter-Roberts Antiques, Inc.
39 Bond Street
New York, NY 10012
(212) 477-9690

The Roycroft Shops
37 South Grove Street
East Aurora, NY 14052
(716) 652-3333

Stickley
1 Stickley Drive
PO Box 480
Manlius, NY 13104-0480
(315) 682-5500
www.stickley.com

Reproduction and modern

Ceramics and tiles

Roycroft Potters
37 South Grove Street
East Aurora, NY 14052
(716) 652-7422

Tile Restoration Center, Inc.
3511 Interlake Avenue North
Seattle, WA 98103
(206) 633-4866

Furniture

Berkeley Mills
2830 7th Street
Berkeley, CA 94710
(510) 549-2854
www.berkeley-mills.com

Darrell Peart
3419 C Street NE #16
Avburn, WA 98002
(425) 277-4070
www.furnituremaker.com

David Berman
Trustworth Studio
PO Box 1109
Plymouth, MA 02362
(508) 746-1847

Prairie Designs of California
PO Box 886
Brisbane, CA 94005
(415) 468-5446

Metalware

Michael Adams
Aurora Studios
3064 County Route 176
Osweto, NY 13126
(315) 343 0339

Arts and Crafts Hardware
28011 Malvina Drive
Warren, MI 48088
(810) 772-7279

Paint

A. Sanderson & Sons Ltd
979 3rd Avenue
Suite 409
New York, NY 10022
(212) 319-7220

David Hellman
86 Highland Avenue
Watertown, MA 02472
(617) 923-4829

Round Valley Iron and Woodworks
PO Box 3744
Bozeman, MT 59772
(406) 582-0929

Stickley
1 Stickley Drive
PO Box 480
Manlius, NY 13104-0480
(315) 682-5500
www.stickley.com

Ted Scherrer
Fairhaven Woodworks
500 Larrabee Avenue
Bellingham, WA 98225
(360) 733-3411

Willow Glen Kitchen & Bath
351 Willow Street
San Jose, CA 95110
(408) 293-2284
www.willowglen.com

Glass/lighting

Arroyo Craftsman
4509 Little John Street
Baldwin Park, CA 91706
(626) 960-9411

Brass Light Gallery
131 South First Street
Milwaukee, WI 53204
(800) 243-9595
www.brasslight.com

Inlight Art Glass
565 Elmwood Avenue
Buffalo, NY 14222
(716) 881-3564

Metro Lighting & Crafts
2121 San Pablo Avenue
Berkeley, CA 94702
(888) 638-7620
www.metrolighting.com

Mica Lamp Co.
517 State Street
Glendale, CA 91203
(818) 241-7227

Rugs

J. R. Burrows & Company
PO Box 522
393 Union Street
Rockland, MA 02370
(781) 982-1812
www.burrows.com

Nancy Thomas
Blue Hills Studio
400 Woodland Way
Greenville, SC 29607
(864) 232-4217

Stained Glass

Glassmasters
2501 Mechanicsville Turnpike
Richmond, VA 23223
(804) 648-4744

Oakbrook Esser Studios
129 East Wisconsin Avenue
Oconomowoc, WI 53066
(262) 567-9310
www.oakbrookesser.com

Stencils

The Stencil Library
Stocksfield Hall
Stocksfield
Northumberland
NE43 7TN
UK
+44 (0)1661 844 844
www.stencil-library.com

Trimbelle River Studio and Design
PO Box 568
Ellsworth, WI 54011
(715) 273-4844

Textiles

Arts and Crafts Period Textiles
5427 Telegraph Avenue #W2
Oakland, CA 94609
(510) 654-1645

J. R. Burrows & Company
PO Box 522
Rockland, MA 02370
(781) 982-1812
www.burrows.com

A. Sanderson & Sons Ltd
979 3rd Avenue
Suite 409
New York, NY 10022
(212) 319-7220

Wallpapers

Charles Rupert
2004 Oak Bay Avenue
Victoria, BC V8R 1E4
Canada

J. R. Burrows & Company
PO Box 522
Rockland, MA 02370
(781) 982-1812
www.burrows.com

A. Sanderson & Sons Ltd
979 3rd Avenue
Suite 409
New York, NY 10022
(212) 319-7220

HOUSES TO VISIT

**Many of these houses have
public tours, but it is wise
to contact them in advance,
just in case they have set times
for viewing.**

USA

Gamble House (Greene & Greene)
4 Westmoreland Place
Pasadena, CA 91103
(626) 793-3334

Mission Inn
3649 Mission Inn Avenue
Riverside, CA 92501
(909) 781-8241

Ennis Browne House (Frank Lloyd
Wright)
2655 Glendower Avenue
Los Angeles, CA 90027
(323) 660-0607

Hollyhock House (Frank
Lloyd Wright)
Barnesdale Art Park
4800 Hollywood Boulevard
Los Angeles, CA 90027
(213) 485-2116

Stickley Museum at
Craftsman Farms (Gustav Stickley)
2352 Route 10 West
Manor Lane
Parsippany-Troy Hills, NJ 07950
(973) 540-1165

Frank Lloyd Wright Home and Studio
951 Chicago Avenue
Oak Park, IL 60302
(708) 848-1976

Roycroft Community
Main and South Grove Streets
East Aurora, NY 14052
(716) 655-0571

Grove Park Inn
290 Macon Avenue
Asheville, NC 28804
(828) 252-2711

UK

Kelmscott Manor (William Morris)
Kelmscott
Nr Lechlade
Gloucestershire GL7 3HJ
(0)1367 252486

Rodmarton Manor (Ernest Barnsley)
Cirencester
Gloucestershire GL7 6PF
(0)1285 841253

Wightwick Manor (Edward Ould with
Morris & Co. interiors)
Wightwick Bank
Nr. Wolverhampton
West Midlands WV6 8EE
(0)1902 761108

Great Maytham Hall (Sir Edwin
Lutyens)
Rolvenden Cranbrook
Kent TN17 4NE
(0)1580 241346

Standen (Philip Webb)
Nr East Grinstead
Sussex RH19 4NE
(0)1342 323029

Blackwell (M. H. Baillie Scott)
Bowness-on-Windermere
Cumbria LA23 3JR
(0)1539 722464

The Hill House (Charles Rennie and
Margaret Mackintosh)
Upper Colquhoun Street
Helensburgh
Argyll and Bute E84 9AJ
(0)1436 673900

Greywalls (Sir Edwin Lutyens)
Muirfield
Gullane
East Lothian EH31 2EF
(0)1620 842144

Melsetter (W.R. Lethaby)
Island of Hoy
Orkney KW16 3M2
(0)1856 791352

INDEX

Numbers in *italics* refer to captions